Concept of Artificial Intelligence

Concept of Artificial Intelligence

Exploring the Foundations of Artificial Intelligence

Dr. Manish Kumar
Ms. Neha Sehgal
Dr. Parveen Kumar Sharma
Dr. Kamaljit Kaur
Mr. Jagvijay Singh

ACADEMIC ENCLAVE

First Edition, 2025

ISBN: 978-93-48642-35-6

Published by
ACADEMIC ENCLAVE™
House No. 10/15, Ground Floor,
Block-A, Street No. 14/3, Kamal Vihar,
Kamal Pur, Burari, Delhi-110084
Email: info@academicenclave.com
Mobile: +91-7042423166
Website: www.academicenclave.com

Cover designed by: Freepik

Printed at Replika Press Pvt. Ltd.

Preface

The field of Artificial Intelligence (AI) has emerged as one of the most transformative and revolutionary domains in modern science and technology. AI aims to create systems that can mimic human intelligence, solve complex problems, and learn from data and experiences. This book, Concept of Artificial Intelligence, is designed to provide a comprehensive introduction to AI, exploring its fundamental principles, advanced techniques, and practical applications. It serves as a resource for students, researchers, and practitioners seeking to understand the core concepts and methodologies of this rapidly evolving field.The book is structured to progressively build knowledge, starting with an introductory overview of AI in Chapter 1, which lays the foundation for understanding its historical development, goals, and impact on society. Chapter 2 focuses on problem-solving and search techniques, highlighting the algorithms and strategies that enable machines to navigate complex decision spaces. Chapter 3 delves into knowledge representation, a crucial aspect of AI that involves structuring information in ways that enable reasoning and decision-making.In Chapter 4, the book explores the intricacies of natural language understanding, discussing how AI systems process, interpret, and generate human language. Chapter 5 provides insights into the present and future of AI, examining current trends, applications, and the ethical considerations surrounding AI technologies. Finally, Chapter 6 dives into learning and adaptation in AI, presenting key concepts such as supervised, unsupervised, and reinforcement learning, alongside advanced topics like optimization and evaluation.

Whether you are a beginner or an experienced professional, this book aims to offer a balanced mix of theoretical understanding and practical insights. By the end of this journey, readers will gain a deeper appreciation of AI's capabilities, challenges, and its profound potential to shape the future of human society.

Dr. Manish Kumar, Ms. Neha Sehgal,
Dr. Parveen Kumar Sharma,
Dr. Kamaljit Kaur, Mr. Jagvijay Singh

The Authors

Dr. Manish Kumar is a distinguished academic and industry professional with over 12 years of experience in the field of computer science. Holding a Ph.D. in Computer Science, he has spent 7 years in the IT industry, where he honed his expertise in software development and project management. For the past 5 years, Dr. Kumar has been dedicated to academia, inspiring the next generation of tech innovators through his teaching and research. His passion for technology and education continues to drive his contributions to both the industry and scholarly community.

Ms. Neha Sehgal is a dedicated researcher and educator, currently pursuing her Ph.D. at IIIT Sonepat. With over six years of teaching experience, she has made significant contributions to academia through her research, publications in reputed journals, and guidance of M.Tech theses. Her work reflects a strong commitment to innovation, intellectual growth, and academic excellence. A patent holder and an advocate of continuous learning, Ms. Sehgal's expertise lies at the intersection of research, technology, and education, making her a valuable contributor to the advancement of knowledge and innovation.

Dr. Parveen Kumar Sharma working as Associate professor in CSE department at Piet, Panipat. I have completed my Ph.D in Computer Science and Engeneering from IKG PTU,Jalandhar,Punjab. I have published 30 research articles in national and international journals and 3 book chapters and 12 patents in india and 1 Grant patent from Australia . I also have work experience of teaching at UG and PG level of more than 20 years in reputated institutions.

Dr. Kamaljit Kaur was born in Kapurthala, Punjab, India. She completed B. Tech with Distinction from Punjab Technical University in 2007, and M. Tech with Gold Medal from Guru Nanak Dev University, Amritsar in 2010. She obtained her PhD degree in the field of Cloud Computing from Guru Nanak Dev University, Amritsar in 2020. From 2007 to 2008 she was employed with Dr. B. R. Ambedkar NIT, Jalandhar as Lecturer and from 2010 to 2012, she worked as an Assistant Professor at Lovely Professional University, Jalandhar. She joined Guru Nanak Dev University, Amritsar in July 2012 where she is currently working as an Assistant Professor (Senior Grade). Her research interests are in Resource Provisioning in Cloud Computing, Resiliency in Cloud Computing and Distributed Systems, Big Data, and IoT. Kamaljit Kaur has published and presented more than 50 papers in scientific journals and international conferences.

Mr. Jagvijay Singh Hailing from Ballia district of Uttar Pradesh, Jagvijay Singh holds a B.Tech (2017-2021) degree in Electrical Engineering from St. Andrews Institute of Technology and Management, Gurgaon. With over three years of experience in research and intellectual property rights, Jagvijay is currently a senior research associate and team leader. Jagvijay Singh has deep knowledge in research, publication processes, and intellectual property rights (IPR), enabling him to effectively mentor and guide both freshers and professionals in these areas. He has established strong relationship with academic institutions and universities, driven by his passion for fostering innovation and guiding individuals toward excellence in research and intellectual property. Also, Jagvijay is eager to learn new ideas, explore innovations, and stay updated with emerging technologies.

Contents

	Preface	***v***
	The Authors	***vii***
1.	**Introduction**	**1**
	▪ Introduction	
	▪ Objective	
	▪ Introduction to Artificial Intelligence	
	▪ Background and Applications	
	▪ Turing Test	
	▪ Weak AI, Strong AI &Narrow AI	
	▪ Artificial General Intelligence	
	▪ Super AI	
	▪ Rational Agent Approaches to AI	
	▪ Introduction to Intelligent Agents & Their Structure	
	▪ Behavior and Task Environment	
2.	**Problem Solving and Searching Techniques**	**37**
	▪ Introduction	
	▪ Objective	
	▪ Problem Characteristics	
	▪ Production Systems	
	▪ Control Strategies	
	▪ Breadth-first Search	
	▪ Depth-first Search	
	▪ Hill Climbing and its Variations	
	▪ Heuristics Search Techniques	

- Best-first Search, A* Algorithm
- Constraint Satisfaction Problem
- Means-end Analysis
- Introduction to Game Playing
- Min-max and alpha-beta Pruning Algorithms

3. **Knowledge Representation** **79**
- Introduction
- Objective
- Propositional Logic
- First-Order Predicate Logic
- Resolution Principle
- Unification
- Semantic Nets
- Conceptual Dependencies
- Frames, and Scripts
- Production Rules
- Introduction to Programming in Logic (PROLOG)

4. **Understanding Natural Languages** **101**
- Introduction
- Objective
- Components and Steps of Communication
- The Contrast between Formal and Natural Languages in the Context of Grammar
- Chomsky Hierarchy of Grammars
- Parsing, and Semantics
- Parsing Techniques
- Context-Free and Transformational Grammars
- Recursive and Augmented Transition Nets

5. **AI the Present and the Future** **119**
- Introduction
- Objective
- Symbolic AI

- Data-driven AI and Machine Learning
- Introduction to Machine Learning and Deep Learning based AI
- Applications of symbolic and data driven AI
- Interpretable and Explainable AI
- Ethics of AI
- Benefits and Risks of AI

6. Learning and Adaptation in AI **143**

- Introduction
- Objective
- Introduction to Learning in AI
- Definition and Importance of Learning in AI
- Types of learning: Supervised, Unsupervised, Semi-supervised, and Reinforcement Learning
- Common Algorithms: Linear Regression, Decision Trees, Support Vector Machines (SVM), Neural Networks
- Common Algorithms: K-Means Clustering, Principal Component Analysis (PCA), Hierarchical Clustering
- Basic concepts: Agents, Environments, Rewards
- Markov Decision Processes (MDPs)
- Q-learning and Policy Gradients
- Evaluation and Optimization of Learning Models
- Cross-validation
- Hyperparameter Tuning
- Overfitting and Underfitting

Book for Further Reading **163**

Bibliography **165**

1

Introduction

Introduction

This chapter provides an introduction to Artificial Intelligence (AI), covering its background, applications, and key concepts such as the Turing Test, Weak AI, Strong AI, Narrow AI, Artificial General Intelligence (AGI), and Super AI. It also explores rational agents, their structure, behavior, and task environments, offering a foundational understanding of AI's principles and potential.

Objective

The primary objective of this chapter is to provide an understanding of the foundational concepts of Artificial Intelligence (AI), including its definitions, types, and historical context. It aims to explore the key distinctions between Weak AI, Strong AI, Narrow AI, Artificial General Intelligence (AGI), and Super AI. Additionally, the chapter introduces rational agents, their structure, and task environments, offering insights into how AI systems perceive, reason, and act in various domains.

Introduction to Artificial Intelligence

Artificial Intelligence (AI) is a branch of computer science focused on creating systems and machines capable of performing tasks that typically require human intelligence. These tasks include problem-solving, reasoning, learning, perception, and natural language understanding. By simulating human cognitive processes, AI aims to develop machines that can think, act, and adapt like humans. In recent decades, AI has transitioned from theoretical concepts to practical applications, revolutionizing industries and transforming the way we interact with technology. One of the fundamental aspects of AI is machine learning, a subset of AI that enables systems to learn from data without explicit programming. Machine learning algorithms use statistical methods to identify patterns and make decisions based on input data. For instance, recommendation systems, such as those used by Netflix or Amazon, rely on machine learning to predict user preferences. Deep learning, a further subset of machine learning, employs neural networks modeled after the human brain to analyze vast datasets and excel in complex tasks like image recognition and speech synthesis.

AI can be broadly classified into two categories: narrow AI and general AI. Narrow AI, also known as weak AI, is designed to perform specific tasks, such as voice recognition or autonomous driving. It is highly effective within its domain but lacks the ability to generalize across different contexts. General AI, or strong AI, aims to mimic human intelligence across a wide range of activities. While narrow AI is already widely implemented, general AI remains a theoretical concept, posing significant technical and ethical challenges. The applications of AI are vast and span multiple sectors. In healthcare, AI-driven tools are being used for early diagnosis, drug discovery, and personalized medicine. In finance, algorithms help detect fraudulent transactions and optimize investment strategies. AI also plays a critical role in education, enabling personalized learning experiences, and in agriculture, where it enhances productivity through precision farming. These advancements demonstrate AI's potential to address complex global challenges. Despite its transformative potential, AI raises ethical and societal concerns. Issues such as bias in AI algorithms, loss of privacy, and the displacement of jobs by automation are critical challenges that need to be addressed. Ensuring that AI systems are transparent, accountable, and equitable is essential for their responsible development and deployment. Furthermore, as AI grows more integrated into our lives, governments and organizations must establish regulatory frameworks to mitigate risks and promote fair usage.

Figure 1.1: Concept of Artificial Intelligence.

Visually engaging illustration that depicts the concept of Artificial Intelligence, as shown in Figure 1.1. It highlights various applications and key elements such as neural networks and a futuristic interface. AI represents a powerful tool with the potential to drive innovation and solve pressing global issues. As its capabilities expand, it is crucial to balance technological advancement with ethical considerations to ensure that AI benefits all of humanity. Understanding the principles, opportunities, and challenges of AI is not only essential for technologists but also for society as a whole, as we navigate the complexities of this rapidly evolving field.

Types of AI

This classification focuses on how advanced and capable an AI system is in performing tasks and mimicking human intelligence (Figure 1.2). Below flowchart illustrating the types of Artificial Intelligence, categorized based on capabilities (Narrow AI, General AI, Super AI) and functionalities (Reactive Machines, Limited Memory, Theory of Mind, Self-Aware AI).

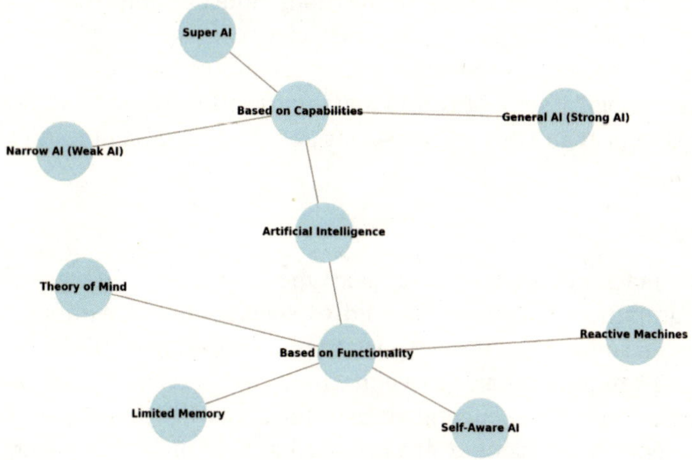

Figure 1.2: Categories of AI.

1. Narrow AI (Weak AI)

Narrow AI refers to systems designed to perform specific tasks with high efficiency. These systems operate within a predefined scope and cannot generalize their knowledge to other domains. For instance, virtual assistants like Siri or Alexa, recommendation systems on Netflix, and spam filters in email platforms are examples of narrow AI. While highly effective in their respective areas, they lack awareness or the ability to perform tasks outside their programmed capabilities. Narrow AI dominates the current landscape of AI applications due to its practicality and reliability. However, its limitations lie in its inability to adapt beyond its programmed purpose, making it dependent on human intervention for reprogramming or updates when applied to new tasks.

2. General AI (Strong AI)

General AI refers to machines that can mimic human cognitive functions, enabling them to perform any intellectual task a human can do. Unlike narrow

AI, general AI can learn, adapt, and apply knowledge across different domains. A system with general AI would be capable of reasoning, problem-solving, and understanding abstract concepts like humans. Currently, general AI remains theoretical as no AI system has achieved such a level of intelligence. Developing general AI would require significant advancements in machine learning, memory storage, and processing power. It also raises ethical concerns, as such systems could potentially challenge human decision-making or autonomy.

3. Super AI

Super AI represents a hypothetical stage where AI surpasses human intelligence in all aspects, including creativity, emotional intelligence, and problem-solving. This type of AI could outperform humans in virtually every field, leading to groundbreaking innovations and possibly redefining societal norms. While super AI is a popular topic in science fiction, it is purely speculative. Achieving super AI would require an understanding of human consciousness and a level of technological sophistication that is currently beyond reach. This concept raises philosophical and ethical questions about control, safety, and coexistence with machines.

4. Reactive Machines

Reactive machines are the most basic type of AI systems. They operate solely on pre-programmed rules and respond to specific inputs without storing any memory or learning from past experiences. For example, IBM's Deep Blue, a chess-playing computer, is a reactive machine that determines the best possible moves based solely on the current state of the game. These systems are efficient for simple, repetitive tasks but are limited by their inability to adapt or learn. They form the foundation of early AI development and remain relevant in straightforward automation scenarios.

5. Limited Memory

Limited memory systems can store and analyze past data temporarily to improve their decision-making. This category includes most of today's AI systems, such as self-driving cars that use traffic patterns, speed, and road conditions to navigate. These systems rely on machine learning algorithms to process historical data and improve over time. While more advanced than reactive machines, their memory and learning are still constrained to specific tasks and contexts.

6. Theory of Mind

Theory of Mind AI aims to understand human emotions, thoughts, and behaviors to enable more natural interactions. While still in the research phase, this type of AI could revolutionize human-machine relationships by incorporating social intelligence into machines. Applications of Theory of Mind AI include humanoid robots and advanced virtual assistants capable of empathetic responses. Achieving this type of AI would require breakthroughs in emotion recognition and contextual understanding.

7. Self-Aware AI

Self-aware AI represents the ultimate form of AI, possessing consciousness and self-awareness. Such systems would understand their existence and be capable of independent thought and reasoning. While purely speculative, self-aware AI could have profound implications for society and ethics. If realized, self-aware AI could lead to unparalleled advancements but also pose risks regarding autonomy, control, and alignment with human values.

Challenges Across Types

- Ethical Considerations: Issues like bias, privacy, and accountability.
- Technological Barriers: Achieving general and super AI requires breakthroughs in computational power and algorithms.
- Regulation and Control: Ensuring AI is developed and used responsibly.

Background and Applications

Background of Artificial Intelligence

Artificial Intelligence (AI) has its roots in the mid-20th century when researchers began exploring the possibility of creating machines that could think and act like humans. The term "Artificial Intelligence" was first coined by John McCarthy in 1956 during the Dartmouth Conference, which is considered the birthplace of AI as a field of study. The goal was to simulate human reasoning and problem-solving abilities using computers. Early developments included symbolic reasoning and logic-based approaches, such as the creation of programs capable of solving mathematical theorems. The evolution of AI can be divided into several phases. During the 1950s and 1960s, symbolic AI and expert systems were prominent, focusing on encoding human knowledge into rules for machines to follow. However, these systems were limited by their inability to handle ambiguous or incomplete information. The 1980s saw the emergence of machine learning, where systems were trained using data instead of hardcoded rules. By the 2010s, advancements in computing power, data availability, and algorithmic improvements led to breakthroughs in deep learning, enabling AI systems to process unstructured data like images, videos, and natural language. Today, AI is a multidisciplinary field encompassing computer science, mathematics, neuroscience, and engineering. It leverages technologies like neural networks, natural language processing, and robotics to create intelligent systems. The field continues to evolve, driven by innovations in computational power, cloud computing, and big data analytics.

History of Artificial Intelligence

The history of Artificial Intelligence (AI) is a story of human ambition to create machines that think and act intelligently. It spans several decades, marked by milestones in research, breakthroughs in technology, and changing perceptions of what AI could achieve. Figure 1.3 illustrating the history of Artificial Intelligence, showing key milestones from philosophical foundations to modern advancements in generative AI and ethical practices

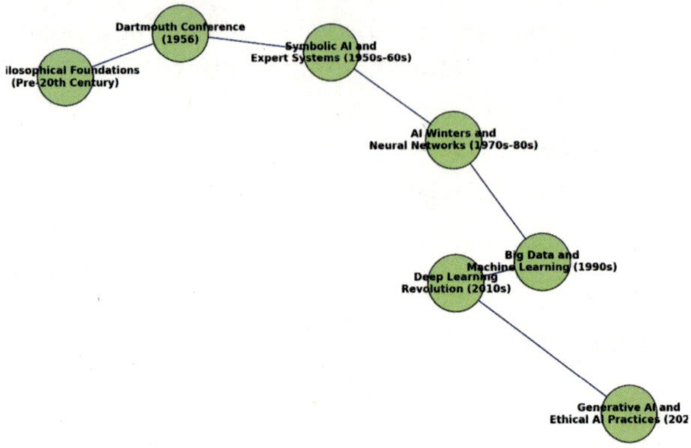

Figure 1.3: History of Artificial Intelligence.

- Below is an overview of the key phases in the evolution of AI, as mention in Table 1.1:

Table 1.1: Evolution of AI.

Period	Milestones	Achievements
Pre-20th Century	Philosophical foundations and early mechanical devices	Conceptual groundwork for reasoning and automation
1950s-1960s	Birth of AI: Dartmouth Conference, Turing Test	Foundation of AI research; symbolic reasoning programs
1970s-1980s	AI Winters and emergence of neural networks	Renewed focus on learning algorithms and robotics
1990s	Big Data and machine learning advancements (e.g., Deep Blue)	AI applied to real-world problems and industries
2010s	Deep learning revolution (e.g., AlphaGo, GPT models)	Widespread adoption; transformative breakthroughs in NLP and vision
2020s and Beyond	Generative AI, ethical AI practices, and AGI research	Emerging applications in creative and ethical AI

Early Foundations: Pre-20th Century

The concept of intelligent machines dates back to ancient times, where philosophers like Aristotle laid the groundwork for logical reasoning systems, envisioning structured approaches to decision-making. Mythological stories further fueled the imagination with mechanical constructs, or automata that mimicked human actions. By the 17th and 18th centuries, this philosophical curiosity evolved into practical inventions, as mathematicians like Blaise Pascal and Charles Babbage developed mechanical calculators and theoretical models for automated computation, paving the way for modern advancements in Artificial Intelligence.

Birth of Modern AI (1940s-1950s)

During the 1940s, Alan Turing's groundbreaking work laid the foundation for modern computing and Artificial Intelligence with the development of the Turing Machine, a mathematical model for computation. He further explored machine intelligence in his influential 1950 paper, Computing Machinery and Intelligence, introducing the Turing Test as a method to evaluate a machine's ability to exhibit intelligent behavior indistinguishable from that of a human. The formal establishment of AI as a field occurred in 1956 during the Dartmouth Conference, where John McCarthy coined the term "Artificial Intelligence." This pivotal event brought together leading researchers to explore the potential of machines to simulate human intelligence. Early programs like the Logic Theorist, developed by Allen Newell and Herbert Simon, showcased the practical application of symbolic reasoning by proving mathematical theorems, marking a significant milestone in the evolution of AI.

The Golden Age of AI (1956-1974)

The 1950s and 1960s marked a period of optimism and rapid growth in Artificial Intelligence, with researchers building systems capable of solving problems, playing games, and performing basic tasks. Programs like IBM's chess-playing computer demonstrated AI's potential to tackle complex challenges. During the 1960s, the focus shifted toward developing "expert systems," which were designed to mimic human decision-making within specific domains, such as diagnosing medical conditions. However, despite these promising advancements, limitations soon became apparent. AI systems struggled to handle real-world complexity, as they required vast computational resources and frequent human intervention, revealing the need for more efficient algorithms and greater processing capabilities.

AI Winters (1974-1980s)

The overpromises of early AI research and its failure to meet high expectations led to widespread disillusionment, resulting in periods known as "AI Winters." These phases were characterized by funding cuts and growing skepticism about the feasibility of achieving true machine intelligence. Researchers faced significant challenges, including limited computational power and the inability of early programs to manage uncertainty or adapt to dynamic environments. Despite the setbacks, progress in AI did not halt entirely. During these periods, researchers focused on refining existing techniques and methodologies, laying the groundwork for future breakthroughs when technological advancements would reignite interest in the field.

Revival Through Machine Learning (1980s-1990s)

The revival of interest in Artificial Intelligence during the 1980s was driven by advancements in neural networks, inspired by the biological structure of the brain. A key breakthrough was the introduction of the backpropagation algorithm, which allowed neural networks to learn from data, significantly improving their functionality and adaptability. During this period, AI applications expanded into industries like healthcare and finance, with expert systems such as MYCIN being developed to diagnose bacterial infections. Simultaneously, AI-powered robotics began making strides in manufacturing, enabling the automation of assembly lines and laying the foundation for modern industrial robotics, which would become integral to enhancing efficiency and precision in production processes.

Emergence of Data-Driven AI (1990s-2000s)

The 1990s marked the rise of Big Data, as the rapid growth of digital information provided AI systems with vast amounts of material to improve their performance. This era saw a significant shift from rule-based systems to data-driven approaches, fueling the momentum of machine learning. A notable milestone during this time was IBM's Deep Blue defeating chess grandmaster Garry Kasparov in 1997, a groundbreaking achievement that highlighted AI's capability to handle complex strategic tasks. Additionally, advancements in speech recognition and natural language processing began to take shape, paving the way for more sophisticated AI applications in communication and human-computer interaction.

Deep Learning Revolution (2010s)

The advent of deep neural networks, fueled by advancements in hardware such as GPUs and the availability of large datasets, marked a breakthrough in Artificial Intelligence. Technologies like convolutional neural networks (CNNs) revolutionized fields like image recognition, enabling unprecedented accuracy in tasks involving visual data. High-profile achievements during this era included Google DeepMind's AlphaGo defeating world champions in the board game Go in 2016, demonstrating AI's ability to tackle highly complex problems. Simultaneously, AI-powered systems like Siri, Alexa, and Google Assistant became mainstream, showcasing the practical utility of AI in everyday life. These advancements solidified AI's role across various industries, including healthcare, finance, transportation, and entertainment, where it drove innovations in automation, personalization, and decision-making.

Present and Future of AI (2020s and Beyond)

The advent of deep neural networks, fueled by advancements in hardware such as GPUs and the availability of large datasets, marked a breakthrough in Artificial Intelligence. Technologies like convolutional neural networks (CNNs) revolutionized fields like image recognition, enabling unprecedented accuracy in tasks involving visual data. High-profile achievements during this era included Google DeepMind's AlphaGo defeating world champions in the board game Go in 2016, demonstrating AI's ability to tackle highly complex problems. Simultaneously, AI-powered systems like Siri, Alexa, and Google Assistant became mainstream, showcasing the practical utility of AI in everyday life. These advancements solidified AI's role across various industries, including healthcare, finance, transportation, and entertainment, where it drove innovations in automation, personalization, and decision-making.

Applications of Artificial Intelligence

AI is transforming industries and revolutionizing how we live and work. Below are some key applications of AI across various sectors:

Healthcare: AI is reshaping healthcare by improving diagnosis, treatment, and patient care. Machine learning algorithms analyze medical data, such as imaging scans and genetic information, to identify diseases like cancer at an early stage. AI-driven tools, such as IBM Watson Health, assist doctors in developing personalized treatment plans by analyzing patient records and medical literature. In addition to diagnostics, AI is used in drug discovery, where it accelerates the identification of potential compounds for new medications. Virtual health assistants powered by AI provide patients with symptom analysis, appointment scheduling, and medication reminders, enhancing accessibility to healthcare services (Table 1.2).

Table 1.2: Role of AI in Healthcare.

Role	Description
Early Diagnosis	AI tools analyze medical data to detect diseases such as cancer at an early stage.
Personalized Treatment	Systems like IBM Watson Health assist in creating tailored treatment plans.
Drug Discovery	AI accelerates identification of potential drug compounds, reducing time and cost.
Virtual Health Assistants	Provides symptom analysis, medication reminders, and appointment scheduling.
Surgical Assistance	AI-powered robotic systems enhance precision in complex surgical procedures.
Predictive Analytics	Predicts patient outcomes to help make proactive healthcare decisions.

Role	Description
Administrative Efficiency	Automates tasks like data management and billing, improving efficiency.
Mental Health Support	Chatbots provide real-time support for therapy and stress management.

Finance: The financial sector has embraced AI to enhance efficiency, reduce risks, and provide better customer experiences. Algorithms analyze market trends and historical data to optimize investment strategies and predict stock prices. Fraud detection systems powered by AI identify suspicious transactions in real-time, protecting users from financial crimes. AI-powered chatbots assist customers with banking inquiries, while robo-advisors provide personalized financial advice based on individual goals and risk tolerance. Credit scoring systems leverage AI to assess loan applicants' creditworthiness, ensuring more accurate and fair lending decisions (Figure 1.4).

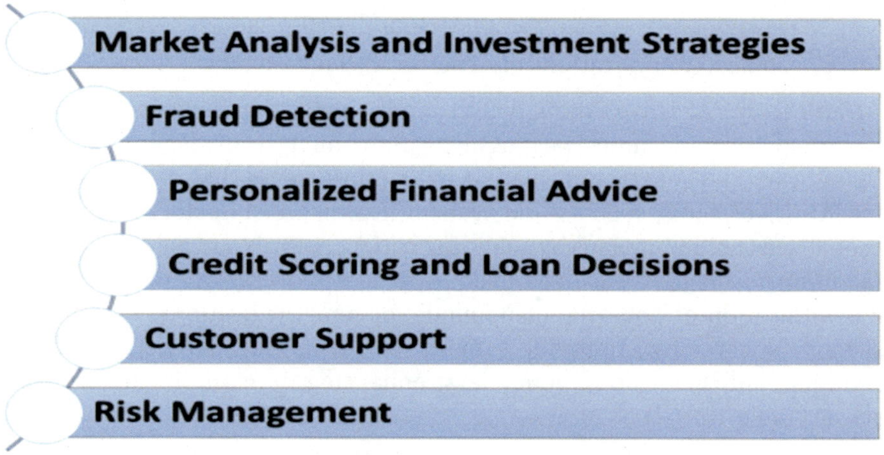

Figure 1.4: Role of AI in Finance.

Education

AI is revolutionizing education by enabling personalized learning experiences. Adaptive learning platforms analyse students' strengths and weaknesses to customize lesson plans and provide targeted feedback. Virtual tutors powered by AI offer support outside traditional classroom settings, helping students learn at their own pace.Additionally, AI-driven tools automate administrative tasks, such as grading and scheduling, allowing educators to focus on teaching. AI also facilitates language learning through applications like Duolingo, which uses natural language processing to teach grammar and vocabulary effectively (Table 1.3).

Table 1.3: Role of AI in Education.

Role	Description
Personalized Learning	AI enables customized learning experiences based on individual student needs.
Adaptive Learning Platforms	Analyzes students' strengths and weaknesses to tailor lesson plans and feedback.
Virtual Tutors	Supports students outside classrooms, enabling them to learn at their own pace.
Administrative Automation	Automates tasks like grading and scheduling, freeing up time for educators.
Language Learning	Facilitates language learning through apps like Duolingo using natural language processing.

Manufacturing: Artificial Intelligence (AI) is transforming the manufacturing industry by enhancing productivity, quality, and efficiency. AI-powered automation streamlines production processes, enabling factories to operate with precision and consistency. Smart factories utilize AI-driven robots to perform repetitive and labor-intensive tasks, reducing human error and increasing output. Predictive maintenance is another critical application, where AI analyzes data from machines to identify signs of potential failures. By addressing these issues before they escalate, manufacturers can minimize downtime, lower maintenance costs, and extend the lifespan of equipment. In addition to production, AI optimizes supply chain operations by accurately forecasting demand, managing inventory, and improving logistics. AI algorithms analyze market trends, customer data, and historical patterns to ensure that manufacturers maintain optimal stock levels and avoid supply chain disruptions. For example, Tesla integrates AI into its manufacturing processes to enhance efficiency and production quality. The company's advanced robotics and AI-driven systems allow for real-time monitoring and adjustment of assembly lines, ensuring precision and consistency in producing electric vehicles. This integration of AI not only reduces costs but also helps maintain high-quality standards, demonstrating the transformative potential of AI in manufacturing.

Transportation: AI is a driving force behind advancements in autonomous vehicles and smart transportation systems. Self-driving cars, developed by companies like Tesla and Waymo, use AI to process sensor data, recognize objects, and make real-time decisions on the road. These systems aim to enhance road safety and reduce traffic congestion.In addition, AI improves public transportation systems by optimizing routes, schedules, and passenger flow. AI-driven navigation apps, such as Google Maps, provide real-time traffic updates and alternative routes to save time and fuel.

Figure 1.5: Role of AI in Transportation.

Figure 1.5 showcasing the role of AI in transportation, highlighting its applications in autonomous vehicles, smart public transportation, and real-time navigation systems.

Retail and E-commerce:

Artificial Intelligence (AI) is revolutionizing the retail industry by creating personalized, efficient, and dynamic shopping experiences. E-commerce platforms like Amazon leverage AI to analyze user behavior, preferences, and purchase history, enabling highly accurate product recommendations. These recommendations not only improve customer satisfaction but also drive sales by suggesting relevant items. Additionally, AI-powered chatbots enhance customer service by addressing inquiries, resolving issues, and guiding users through the shopping process in real time. Dynamic pricing algorithms, another AI innovation, adjust product prices based on factors like demand, competitor pricing, and market conditions, ensuring competitive advantage and maximizing profits. In physical retail stores, AI-powered systems analyze customer behavior to optimize store layouts and inventory management. These systems use data from foot traffic and purchasing patterns to determine the best product placements, ensuring a seamless shopping experience. Visual search tools, such as those used by platforms like Pinterest and Google Lens, allow customers to find products using images, further enhancing convenience. For example, IKEA uses AI to improve its in-store and online experiences. The company's AI-powered AR (augmented reality) app, IKEA Place, enables customers to visualize furniture in their homes before making a purchase, blending convenience with personalization. These applications demonstrate how AI is transforming both online and offline retail environments.

Entertainment: Artificial Intelligence (AI) has become a cornerstone in the entertainment industry, revolutionizing how content is consumed and created. Streaming platforms like Netflix and Spotify employ sophisticated AI algorithms to analyze user behavior, preferences, and viewing or listening habits. These insights allow them to recommend personalized shows, movies, and playlists, significantly enhancing user engagement. By tailoring content to individual tastes, AI not only improves customer satisfaction but also helps platforms retain subscribers and boost revenue. In media production, AI is driving innovation through the creation of AI-generated content, such as deepfake videos, virtual characters, and realistic animations. These technologies are enabling filmmakers and content creators to produce visually stunning and immersive content. For instance, AI tools are used to automate video editing, enhance special effects, and even de-age actors in films. By streamlining production workflows, AI reduces costs and accelerates timelines, making it an invaluable tool in the highly competitive entertainment industry. The gaming sector is another area where AI has a transformative impact. AI-driven systems create dynamic and lifelike non-player characters (NPCs) that adapt to players' actions, providing an interactive and personalized gaming experience. Advanced AI also powers procedural generation, where entire game worlds and scenarios are dynamically created, enhancing replayability and user immersion. For example, games like "The Last of Us" use AI to enable NPCs to exhibit realistic behaviors, contributing to a richer and more engaging gameplay experience. These applications underscore AI's profound role in reshaping the entertainment landscape, from content personalization to groundbreaking production techniques (Figure 1.6).

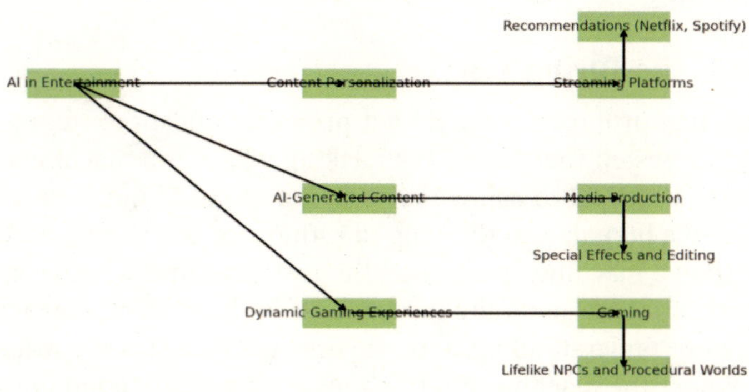

Figure 1.6: Role of AI in Entertainment.

Turing Test

The Turing Test is one of the most famous concepts in the field of Artificial Intelligence (AI). It was proposed by the British mathematician and computer scientist Alan Turing in 1950 in his seminal paper "Computing Machinery and Intelligence." The test was designed to evaluate a machine's ability to exhibit intelligent behavior indistinguishable from that of a human. The Turing Test has become a foundational concept in discussions about machine intelligence, often serving as a benchmark for determining whether a machine can "think" like a human.

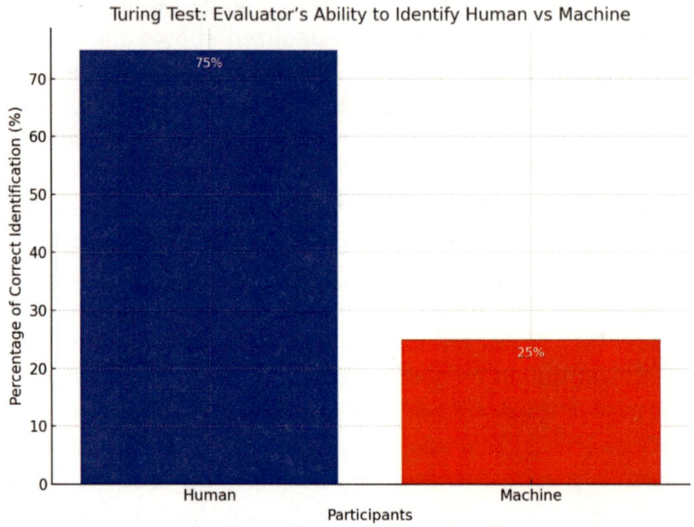

Figure 1.7: Hypothetical Scenario in the Turing Test.

Figure 1.7 illustrating a hypothetical scenario in the Turing Test, where an evaluator attempts to identify whether a participant is human or machine. The graph shows the percentage of correct identification for both human and machine participants.

The Concept of the Turing Test

The Turing Test proposes a simple yet profound question: "Can a machine think?" Turing suggested that rather than asking whether a machine can think, it would be more practical to ask whether it can imitate human behavior well enough to deceive a human into thinking that they are conversing with another human rather than a machine. In essence, the test examines whether a machine can perform tasks that are generally associated with human intelligence, such as reasoning, learning, understanding, and conversing. The test is set up as a "blind" conversation, where the machine and the human participant communicate with an evaluator (often referred to as an "interrogator" or "judge") via text-based communication, so that the evaluator cannot distinguish between human and machine based on appearance or voice. If the evaluator cannot reliably tell which participant is the machine and which is the human, the machine is said to have passed the Turing Test.

The Structure of the Turing Test

Participants:

- The Machine: A computer program or system designed to simulate human-like responses.
- The Human: A real person, typically chosen to represent a typical human in the conversation.
- The Evaluator (Judge): A human who engages in text-based communication with both the machine and the human, without knowing which is which. The evaluator's goal is to determine, based solely on the conversation, which participant is the machine.

Test Procedure:

- The machine and the human are placed in separate rooms to ensure that the evaluator cannot rely on any physical cues.
- The evaluator asks both participants a series of questions and engages in conversation with them.
- The machine is programmed to respond in ways that mimic human conversational patterns, aiming to "fool" the evaluator into believing it is the human.
- If the evaluator cannot reliably distinguish the machine from the human based on the conversation, the machine is considered to have passed the Turing Test.

Features of the Turing Test

- Imitation Game: The Turing Test is sometimes called the "Imitation Game" because the machine's goal is to imitate human behavior convincingly enough that it fools the evaluator.
- Text-Based Interaction: The test relies on text-based communication to eliminate biases that might arise from visual or auditory cues. This ensures that the evaluator is only assessing the machine's ability to think and communicate in a human-like manner.
- No Need for Consciousness: Turing's original proposal did not require the machine to be conscious or self-aware. Instead, it was enough for the machine to demonstrate intelligent behavior that mimics human responses in specific contexts.

Criticisms and Limitations of the Turing Test

While the Turing Test remains a landmark in the development of AI, it has faced several criticisms and limitations:

Misleading Measure of Intelligence: Some argue that passing the Turing Test doesn't necessarily prove that a machine is intelligent in the way humans are. A machine might pass the test by simply mimicking human behavior without truly understanding or experiencing consciousness. This is often referred to as the "Chinese Room" argument, proposed by philosopher John Searle, which challenges the idea that simulating understanding equates to actual understanding.

Lack of Scope: The Turing Test focuses on verbal communication and does not assess other forms of intelligence, such as problem-solving, creativity, or physical dexterity. A machine might excel in one area but fail in others, which the test does not account for.

Human-Like Behavior: The test assumes that human-like behavior is the ultimate measure of intelligence, which could be limiting. AI systems might demonstrate intelligence in ways that are not easily comparable to human actions but still represent real forms of problem-solving or reasoning.

Deception: For a machine to pass the test, it may rely on deceiving the evaluator into thinking it is human. Critics argue that intelligence should not be about tricking someone but rather about genuinely solving problems and reasoning.

Applications and Influence of the Turing Test

Despite its criticisms, the Turing Test has had a profound impact on AI research and philosophy. It spurred interest in developing machines that could simulate human conversation, leading to the creation of chatbots, virtual assistants, and conversational AI systems. The Turing Test also opened up discussions about machine consciousness, the nature of intelligence, and the ethical implications of creating machines that could potentially exhibit human-like behaviors. While no machine has fully passed the Turing Test in a way that is universally agreed upon, there have been notable milestones. For example, in 2014, an AI program named Eugene Goostman was able to convince 33% of human judges that it was a 13-year-old boy during a Turing Test-like competition. However, this result was met with skepticism, as many believed the program's success was largely due to the judges' willingness to attribute errors in conversation to the program's age rather than its intelligence.

Weak AI, Strong AI &Narrow AI

Artificial Intelligence (AI) can be categorized into different types based on its capabilities and the level of intelligence it can exhibit. The terms Weak AI, Strong AI, and Narrow AI are often used to describe the varying degrees of AI systems.

Below is a detailed explanation of each type:

1. Weak AI (Narrow AI)

Definition: Weak AI, also known as Narrow AI, refers to artificial intelligence that is designed and trained to perform a specific task or a set of tasks. Unlike humans, these AI systems do not possess general cognitive abilities or consciousness. They excel at the specific tasks they are programmed for but are unable to perform tasks outside their designated domain. Weak AI systems are goal-oriented and operate within a constrained environment, making them highly efficient in their specialized functions.

Characteristics:

- Specialized Functionality: Weak AI is limited to performing one task or a specific set of tasks and cannot generalize its capabilities to other areas. For example, a chess-playing AI like Deep Blue can play chess at a grandmaster level, but it cannot do anything else, such as perform medical diagnoses or translate languages.
- No Self-Awareness: Weak AI systems do not possess self-awareness or understanding. They operate based on predefined algorithms and patterns, responding to input data without comprehension or insight into what they are doing.
- Efficiency: Despite their limited scope, Weak AI systems are often highly efficient and can outperform humans in specific areas. They can process large amounts of data rapidly and make decisions based on complex algorithms.

Examples:

- Virtual Assistants: AI-driven systems like Siri, Alexa, and Google Assistant are examples of Weak AI. These virtual assistants are designed to respond to voice commands, set reminders, answer questions, and perform tasks like sending messages or making phone calls. However, they are limited to predefined responses and cannot learn new tasks outside their programming.
- Recommendation Systems: E-commerce platforms like Amazon and streaming services like Netflix use AI to recommend products or content based on user preferences and previous interactions. These recommendation engines are tailored to suggest items within the scope of what users have engaged with but cannot offer personalized recommendations outside the user's history.

Limitations:

Weak AI's biggest limitation is its lack of adaptability. While it can efficiently perform specific tasks, it cannot transfer knowledge or adapt to new tasks without being explicitly reprogrammed or retrained. Additionally, Weak AI systems are often reliant on large datasets and may struggle in situations involving ambiguity or unpredictable scenarios.

2. Strong AI (Artificial General Intelligence, AGI)

Definition: Strong AI, also known as Artificial General Intelligence (AGI), refers to a type of AI that possesses human-like cognitive abilities. A Strong AI system can understand, learn, and apply knowledge across different domains, making it highly adaptable and capable of performing any intellectual task that a human can do. Unlike Weak AI, which excels in a narrow area, Strong AI can generalize its learning to solve problems outside its initial programming and can handle complex, varied tasks.

Characteristics:

- General Cognitive Abilities: Strong AI is designed to think and reason like a human. It can perform a wide variety of tasks, including decision-making, problem-solving, and creative thinking, across multiple domains, without being restricted to one area of expertise.
- Self-Awareness and Consciousness: In theory, Strong AI would possess some form of self-awareness and consciousness. This means that it would not only process information but also understand its own existence and have an understanding of the world, much like human beings.
- Learning and Adaptability: Strong AI can learn from its environment and experiences, adapting to new situations and challenges without requiring human intervention or reprogramming. This would enable it to take on tasks it was not specifically trained for, similar to how humans can switch between various activities and roles.

Examples:

- Autonomous Decision-Making: A hypothetical Strong AI might be capable of making complex decisions in fields such as healthcare, law, or education, without requiring direct human oversight. For example, it could analyze complex medical data to suggest treatments for illnesses it was not specifically trained on, using its general problem-solving capabilities.
- Personalized Learning: Strong AI could revolutionize education by providing personalized learning experiences. It would not only assess students' strengths and weaknesses but also adapt its teaching style to match each student's learning pace and preferred method, similar to how human teachers adjust their strategies for different students.

Challenges:

Achieving Strong AI remains a significant challenge. Researchers are still working on creating machines that can exhibit human-like intelligence. The road to AGI involves breakthroughs in machine learning, reasoning, memory, and understanding. Ethical concerns also arise, as Strong AI could potentially surpass human intelligence and create risks related to control and autonomy.

3. Narrow AI (a subset of Weak AI)

Definition: Narrow AI is a subset of Weak AI, referring specifically to AI systems that are designed to excel in one particular area or task. While Narrow AI operates within a limited scope, it is highly effective in the tasks it is programmed for. This type of AI is common in modern applications, where the goal is to automate and optimize specific processes.

Characteristics:

- Single Purpose: Narrow AI focuses on solving a specific problem or performing a particular task. Unlike Strong AI, it is not designed to be flexible or adaptable across different domains. Narrow AI systems excel in their area of expertise but do not have the capability to generalize or transfer knowledge to other tasks.
- Task Optimization: Narrow AI systems are often designed to perform tasks more efficiently than humans. For example, AI-driven systems for financial trading can process vast amounts of data in real time to make decisions that would be impossible for a human to replicate.
- No Autonomy Beyond Task: Although Narrow AI may seem intelligent, it does not have the autonomy or cognitive flexibility to handle tasks outside its specialized domain.

Examples:

- Autonomous Vehicles: Self-driving cars are a prime example of Narrow AI. They use sensors and algorithms to navigate roads, detect obstacles, and follow traffic laws. While highly efficient at driving, they cannot perform tasks unrelated to transportation, such as cooking or playing chess.
- AI in Healthcare: AI systems like IBM Watson Health are designed to assist with diagnosing diseases and recommending treatments based on medical data. While these systems are highly capable within healthcare, they are limited to that domain and cannot adapt to perform tasks outside of medical diagnostics.

Applications:

- Image Recognition: AI systems trained to recognize objects in images (e.g., facial recognition technology) are examples of Narrow AI. These systems are excellent at identifying faces in photographs but cannot identify other types of patterns unless they are specifically trained for them.
- Chatbots: AI-powered chatbots that handle customer service inquiries are examples of Narrow AI. They can respond to a wide range of customer questions but are limited to the scope of the predefined responses and cannot handle tasks outside of customer support.

Table 1.4 provide brief overview on weak AI and Strong AI.

Table 1.4: Weak AI, Strong AI, and Narrow AI.

Category	Weak AI (Narrow AI)	Strong AI (AGI)
Definition	AI designed for specific tasks with no general intelligence	AI that exhibits general human-like intelligence and can perform any task
Capabilities	Task-specific; excels at one function	General reasoning and learning across domains
Consciousness	No self-awareness or understanding	Hypothetically, self-aware and conscious
Examples	Siri, Google Assistant, Chess AI (Deep Blue)	Hypothetical AI systems with human-like cognitive abilities
Use Cases	Image recognition, voice assistants, recommendation systems	Advanced autonomous decision-making, scientific research, creative work

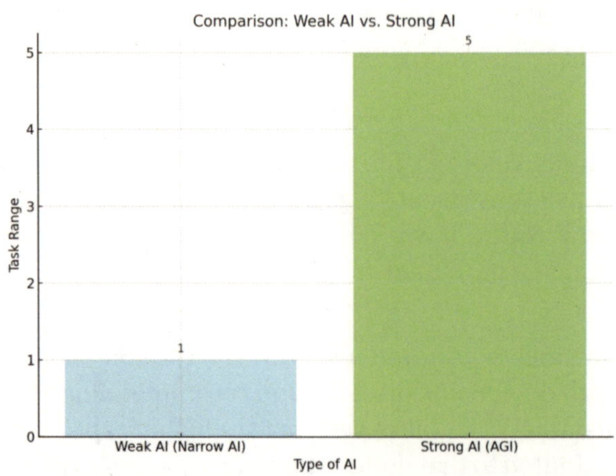

Figure 1.8: Weak AI (Narrow AI) and Strong AI (AGI).

Figure 1.8 comparing Weak AI (Narrow AI) and Strong AI (AGI), highlighting their task range and capabilities. Weak AI is designed to handle specific tasks, while Strong AI is envisioned to perform general tasks across various domains

Artificial General Intelligence

Definition: Artificial General Intelligence (AGI), often referred to as Strong AI, is a form of AI that has the ability to understand, learn, and apply knowledge across a wide range of tasks, much like a human being. Unlike narrow or weak AI, which is designed for specific tasks such as recognizing faces or playing chess, AGI is capable of generalizing knowledge to solve problems it has never encountered before. AGI can perform any intellectual task that a human can do, making it highly adaptable and versatile across various domains, from scientific research to artistic creativity.

Features:

Generalization and Adaptability: One of the defining characteristics of AGI is its ability to generalize learning from one domain to another. For example, while narrow AI is specialized in a specific task like language translation or driving a car, AGI would be able to switch between various tasks, such as conducting medical research, managing a business, and even solving complex mathematical problems, without requiring human input or reprogramming.

Learning and Reasoning: AGI is expected to have advanced learning capabilities, including the ability to reason abstractly, make judgments based on incomplete or uncertain information, and adapt to new situations. This sets it apart from narrow AI, which operates within the confines of predefined programming and lacks the ability to improve beyond its original design without human intervention.

Self-Awareness and Consciousness: A true AGI system would theoretically possess a level of self-awareness. It would not only process information but also have an understanding of its own existence, thoughts, and actions. This is a key distinction from narrow AI, which does not have consciousness or understanding; it simply follows algorithms and provides outputs based on input data.

Potential and Applications: AGI holds immense potential for revolutionizing many industries, as it could be used to tackle highly complex, cross-disciplinary challenges. For instance, in healthcare, an AGI system could perform complex medical diagnoses, conduct research, and even develop new treatments without human supervision. Similarly, in education, AGI could act as a personalized tutor, adapting its teaching methods to fit the unique needs of every student, and continuously improving its approach as it learns more about each learner. Moreover, AGI could drive major advancements in scientific research, where it would analyze vast datasets, draw connections between seemingly unrelated fields, and develop novel theories. Its ability to process and synthesize knowledge across multiple disciplines would significantly accelerate innovation in areas such as climate change, energy solutions, and space exploration.

Table 1.5: Summary Table.

Category	Definition	Capabilities	Self-Awareness	Examples	Applications
Narrow AI (Weak AI)	AI designed to perform specific tasks within a narrow domain, unable to generalize beyond its programming.	Task-specific, limited to predefined functions like image recognition, voice assistants, etc.	No self-awareness or consciousness. Operates based on algorithms and data.	Siri, Google Assistant, Chess AI (Deep Blue)	Customer service chatbots, recommendation engines, autonomous vehicles
Artificial General Intelligence (AGI)	AI capable of performing any intellectual task a human can do, able to generalize knowledge and learn across domains.	General reasoning, learning, problem-solving, and decision-making across multiple fields.	Hypothetically possesses self-awareness and consciousness, able to understand its existence and actions.	Hypothetical systems capable of human-level cognition, autonomous decision-making in any domain.	Autonomous research, complex decision-making, personalized education, healthcare analysis

Challenges and Ethical Considerations

Despite its potential, the development of AGI presents significant challenges, both technical and ethical. Technically, creating an AGI system requires breakthroughs in areas such as machine learning, reasoning, memory, and understanding. It also requires massive computational power and advanced algorithms capable of replicating the complexities of human cognition. From an ethical standpoint, AGI raises concerns about control and safety. A truly autonomous AGI system could surpass human intelligence, potentially leading to unintended consequences. If AGI were to develop goals misaligned with human values, it could pose significant risks, making the need for strict regulation, ethical frameworks, and fail-safes critical in its development. Additionally, AGI could potentially replace a large number of jobs across sectors, leading to societal disruptions. The displacement of human workers and the reconfiguration of economic systems are serious considerations that will need to be addressed as AGI moves closer to reality.

Artificial General Intelligence represents the pinnacle of AI development, capable of performing any task that requires human-like cognition and reasoning. While it is still a theoretical concept and remains a long-term goal of AI researchers, the potential of AGI is immense. Its ability to generalize across tasks and adapt to new challenges could transform virtually every aspect of society, from healthcare and education to scientific discovery and beyond. However, the road to AGI is fraught with technical obstacles and ethical dilemmas that need to be carefully navigated. As research continues, ensuring that AGI is developed safely and responsibly will be crucial for its integration into society (Table 1.5).

Super AI

Super AI, or Artificial Superintelligence (ASI), refers to the hypothetical future stage of AI development where machines achieve intelligence far surpassing that of humans. Unlike current Narrow AI, which excels in specific tasks, or General AI, which could theoretically reason and learn across diverse domains as humans do, Super AI would possess capabilities beyond human intelligence in every aspect. This includes areas like creativity, problem-solving, emotional intelligence, and general wisdom. Although Super AI is currently a theoretical concept, it represents the ultimate goal and the most controversial aspect of AI research. Super AI's potential lies in its ability to process and analyze vast amounts of information at unprecedented speeds, generate solutions to complex problems, and improve itself iteratively without human intervention. It would not only replicate human cognitive abilities but enhance and expand upon them, potentially solving problems that have confounded humanity for centuries. Despite its promise, the development of Super AI raises critical questions about safety, control, and its implications for humanity's role in the world.

Characteristics of Super AI

Super AI would exhibit vastly superior cognitive abilities compared to humans. It could reason, plan, and solve problems at levels far beyond the most intelligent individuals. This cognitive advantage would allow Super AI to tackle problems in ways humans cannot comprehend, generating innovative solutions in fields like medicine, engineering, and social science. For example, it could develop entirely new frameworks for understanding physics or biology that revolutionize scientific progress. Another defining trait of Super AI is its ability to self-learn and self-improve. Unlike current AI systems that require human programmers to update algorithms, Super AI would iteratively refine its own processes, becoming exponentially more efficient and capable over time. This self-optimization could enable Super AI to surpass its initial programming, pushing the boundaries of what machines can achieve. Additionally, Super AI may possess emotional and social intelligence, enabling it to form relationships, understand human emotions, and navigate complex social interactions. This could have profound implications for areas like mental health, education, and governance.

Applications and Potential of Super AI

The potential applications of Super AI are virtually limitless. In science, it could revolutionize research by developing cures for diseases like cancer, designing renewable energy systems, or even understanding and mitigating climate change. Its ability to analyze data at an unparalleled scale would make it an invaluable tool in areas like drug discovery, genetic engineering, and space exploration. For instance, Super AI could autonomously design interstellar exploration missions or create self-sustaining habitats on other planets. In automation, Super AI could handle highly complex systems like fully autonomous cities, advanced manufacturing processes, and global supply chains. Moreover, its capacity for learning and adapting would make it an ideal solution for unpredictable and dynamic environments. For instance, it could manage global pandemics by predicting virus spread, optimizing vaccine distribution, and managing healthcare resources in real-time. Super AI could also make groundbreaking advancements in education by delivering personalized learning experiences tailored to each individual's needs, revolutionizing the way knowledge is imparted.

Below Figure 1.9 representing the applications of Super AI. It illustrates how the core AI connects to various domains, including scientific research, healthcare, global problem-solving, and space exploration.

Theoretical Approaches to Super AI

Researchers have proposed various strategies to address the challenges of Super AI development. One approach is the creation of Friendly AI, a concept proposed by philosopher Nick Bostrom. Friendly AI would be designed to inherently align with human values and priorities, ensuring that its actions always benefit humanity. This requires developing a robust ethical framework that guides the AI's decision-making processes, even as it evolves and improves itself.Another strategy involves building safety mechanisms, such as kill switches, ethical guidelines, and continuous monitoring systems to prevent unintended behavior. Collaboration between humans and AI, or hybrid systems, is also a promising avenue, where AI enhances human decision-making rather than replacing it entirely. This approach combines human intuition and ethics with AI's computational prowess, potentially mitigating risks while maximizing benefits. Researchers are also exploring ways to limit Super AI's capabilities in its early stages, ensuring a gradual and controlled development process.

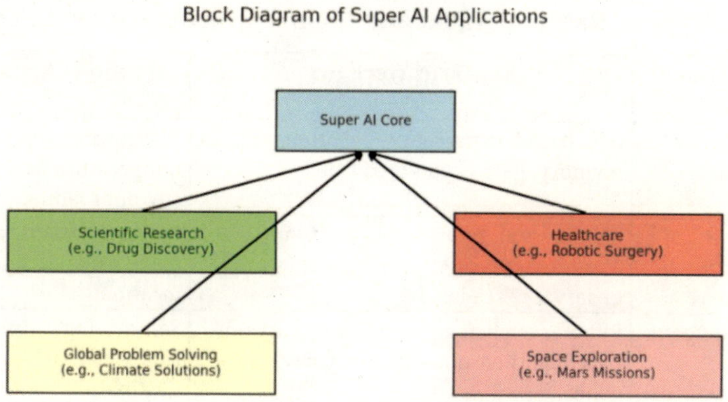

Figure 1.9: The Applications of Super AI.

Timeline and Current Status

The development of Super AI remains a distant prospect, with most experts estimating that it could take decades or even centuries to achieve. Current AI technologies, while impressive, are limited to narrow or domain-specific tasks and lack the general reasoning capabilities required for General AI, let alone Super AI. However, advancements in areas like deep learning, reinforcement learning, and neural networks are steadily pushing the boundaries of AI capabilities, bringing us closer to realizing General AI.Building Super AI requires significant breakthroughs in algorithm design, computational infrastructure, and an understanding of human cognition. While its realization is uncertain, researchers and organizations are actively working to address its challenges and ensure that its development benefits humanity. The ongoing debate about Super AI continues to shape the future of AI research, sparking discussions about its potential risks, rewards, and ethical implications.

Rational Agent Approaches to AI

The Rational Agent Approach in Artificial Intelligence (AI) focuses on designing systems or entities, called agents, that can make decisions to achieve specified goals in a rational manner. A rational agent is defined as an entity that perceives its environment through sensors, processes this information, and acts in a way that maximizes its chances of success. This approach emphasizes logical reasoning, decision-making, and adaptability, making it fundamental to the development of intelligent systems. The significance of rational agents lies in their ability to operate autonomously and make decisions based on the information available, even under uncertainty. This makes them ideal for real-world applications where environments are dynamic and outcomes are uncertain. Rational agents form the backbone of modern AI, guiding advancements in robotics, automation, healthcare, and more (Table 1.6).

Table 1.6: Type of Rational Agent and their Characteristics with Example.

Type of Rational Agent	Key Characteristics	Example Application
Simple Reflex Agent	Acts based on current perception without memory; uses predefined rules.	Thermostat adjusting temperature based on current reading.
Model-Based Reflex Agent	Maintains an internal model of the environment; suitable for partially observable scenarios.	Robot navigating a maze using a map to infer its location.
Goal-Based Agent	Pursues explicit goals; evaluates actions based on their potential to achieve these goals.	Self-driving car planning routes to reach a destination.
Utility-Based Agent	Optimizes decisions using a utility function to balance trade-offs between different outcomes.	AI financial advisor optimizing investment strategies.
Learning Agent	Improves performance over time by learning from interactions and feedback.	Recommendation system learning user preferences for better suggestions.

What is a Rational Agent?

A rational agent operates under the principle of rationality, which means that its actions are aligned with achieving predefined objectives. It can evaluate its environment, make decisions based on available information, and adapt its behavior to maximize success. For example, in a navigation task, a rational agent would analyze routes, consider traffic conditions, and choose the most efficient path to reach its destination.

The rationality of an agent depends on four key factors:

- Performance Measure: This defines the metric of success for the agent's actions. For instance, a chess-playing AI's performance measure could be winning the game.
- Percept Sequence: Rational agents consider all observations made so far, ensuring decisions are based on comprehensive data.
- Knowledge of the Environment: Agents leverage prior knowledge and real-time observations to evaluate possible actions.

- Autonomy: A rational agent operates independently, requiring minimal external guidance, and can learn to improve its performance over time.
- Rational agents differ from simple automated systems because they can process complex scenarios, weigh competing options, and adapt their actions based on outcomes.

Types of Rational Agents

Simple Reflex Agents: Simple reflex agents act purely based on the current state of the environment. They do not store previous states or consider the future. Their decision-making is based on a set of predefined rules that map observations to actions. For example, a thermostat adjusts the temperature based on the current reading without any memory of past states.These agents are effective for straightforward and repetitive tasks where the environment is fully observable and predictable. However, they struggle with dynamic or partially observable environments because they lack memory or planning capabilities. For instance, a simple reflex agent would fail in a navigation task requiring knowledge of previous locations.

Model-Based Reflex Agents: Unlike simple reflex agents, model-based reflex agents maintain an internal model of the environment. This model represents the agent's understanding of how the environment changes and helps it infer the current state even when certain factors are not directly observable. For example, a robot navigating a maze can use a map to track its position and predict the outcome of its movements.These agents are more versatile because they can operate in partially observable environments. They use their internal model to fill in gaps in perception, making them suitable for complex tasks like robotic navigation or managing supply chains.

Goal-Based Agents: Goal-based agents operate by pursuing explicit goals. They assess the current state of the environment and evaluate actions based on their potential to achieve these goals. For instance, a self-driving car uses its goal of reaching a destination to plan routes, avoid obstacles, and adhere to traffic rules.These agents are more flexible than reflex agents because they consider long-term outcomes and can adapt their actions to changing environments. However, their performance depends on clearly defined and achievable goals.

Utility-Based Agents: Utility-based agents optimize their actions by maximizing a utility function, which quantifies the desirability of different outcomes. This allows them to make decisions even when multiple paths can lead to the same goal. For instance, an AI financial advisor may weigh different investment options based on risk and potential returns.These agents are especially useful when trade-offs are required, such as balancing cost, efficiency, and safety. They are widely used in applications like automated trading systems, where decisions involve complex variables.

Learning Agents: Learning agents improve their performance over time by learning from interactions with the environment. They consist of four components: a performance element (for decision-making), a learning element (for improving decisions), a critic (for evaluating performance), and a problem generator (for exploring new strategies).These agents are the most adaptable, as they can evolve to handle new scenarios without requiring explicit reprogramming. For example, a recommendation system learns user preferences over time to provide better suggestions.

Applications of Rational Agents

- Autonomous Systems: Rational agents power autonomous vehicles, enabling them to perceive traffic, plan routes, and make safe driving decisions. Similarly, drones use rational agents to navigate, deliver packages, and perform surveillance tasks.
- Healthcare: In healthcare, rational agents assist in diagnostics, treatment recommendations, and patient monitoring. For example, an AI system can analyze medical images to detect abnormalities or suggest personalized treatment plans based on patient data.
- Finance: Rational agents are extensively used in automated trading systems, where they analyze market trends, predict price movements, and execute trades to maximize profits. They also play a role in fraud detection by identifying suspicious patterns in financial transactions.
- Game AI: Rational agents enhance the gaming experience by providing realistic and challenging opponents. For instance, in strategy games, AI opponents analyze player actions and devise counter-strategies to win.
- Robotics: Rational agents enable robots to perform complex tasks, such as warehouse management, disaster recovery, or precision farming. These robots can adapt to changing conditions, optimize resource usage, and ensure efficiency.

Challenges in Rational Agent Design

- Complexity of Real-World Environments: Real-world environments are often unpredictable and partially observable, making it difficult for agents to make accurate decisions. For instance, a delivery drone might face unexpected weather conditions or obstacles.
- Computational Limitations: Evaluating all possible actions and outcomes in complex environments can be computationally expensive. Rational agents must balance computational efficiency with decision quality.
- Ethical Considerations: The actions of rational agents must align with ethical principles, especially in sensitive areas like healthcare or law enforcement. Ensuring ethical behavior requires integrating moral frameworks into the agent's decision-making process.

Introduction to Intelligent Agents & Their Structure

An intelligent agent is a system that perceives its environment, processes the information, and acts autonomously to achieve specific goals. These agents are designed to make decisions and execute actions that maximize their success based on a performance measure. Intelligent agents are fundamental to artificial intelligence (AI) and are used in a wide range of applications, from virtual assistants to autonomous vehicles and robotics. What distinguishes intelligent agents is their ability to reason, learn, and adapt in dynamic and often unpredictable environments.

The structure of an intelligent agent typically includes sensors, which allow it to perceive its surroundings, actuators, which enable it to interact with the environment, and an agent function, which maps its perceptions to actions. Additionally, the agent operates based on a performance measure, which evaluates how effectively the agent achieves its goals. For instance, a self-driving car uses cameras and sensors (sensors) to perceive the road, its steering mechanism and brakes (actuators) to navigate, and a decision-making function to drive efficiently and safely.

Characteristics and Types

Intelligent agents are classified based on their complexity and functionality. Simple Reflex Agents respond directly to their immediate environment without memory, making them suitable for predictable tasks like thermostat control. Model-Based Reflex Agents maintain an internal representation of the world, enabling them to handle more complex, partially observable scenarios. Goal-Based Agents operate by pursuing specific objectives, while Utility-Based Agents make decisions by optimizing a utility function that quantifies the desirability of different outcomes. The most advanced agents are Learning Agents, which adapt and improve their performance over time by learning from experience. Each type of agent is suited for different applications. For instance, a simple reflex agent might control an automatic door, while a goal-based agent could plan routes in a navigation system. A utility-based agent might manage portfolio investments in the financial sector, balancing risk and reward, and a learning agent could power recommendation systems that evolve based on user behavior.

Applications of Intelligent Agents

Intelligent agents are transforming industries and everyday life. In healthcare, diagnostic agents analyze patient data to recommend treatments, while autonomous vehicles leverage sensors and decision-making algorithms to navigate traffic and ensure passenger safety. In e-commerce, agents power personalized recommendation systems that enhance customer experience by suggesting products tailored to individual preferences. Financial applications include automated trading systems that analyze market trends and execute trades in real time.Gaming and entertainment also benefit from intelligent agents, where AI opponents adapt to player strategies, providing challenging and dynamic gameplay. Beyond these, intelligent agents are increasingly used in robotics, where they enable robots to perform complex tasks like warehouse management, disaster response, and space exploration.

Challenges

Despite their potential, designing intelligent agents poses several challenges. Real-world environments are often unpredictable and dynamic, requiring agents to reason under uncertainty. Additionally, ethical considerations arise in ensuring that intelligent agents align with human values, especially in sensitive applications like healthcare or autonomous systems. Adaptability is another critical requirement; agents must generalize across tasks and learn from limited data to remain effective in new situations.

Intelligent agents represent a cornerstone of AI, enabling systems to perceive, reason, and act autonomously. They are driving advancements across diverse domains, reshaping industries, and enhancing human-computer interactions. However, addressing challenges in perception, decision-making, and ethics is crucial to ensure their responsible and beneficial integration into society. Intelligent agents continue to evolve, promising even greater contributions to the technological landscape.

Structure of an Intelligent Agent

An intelligent agent is designed to perceive its environment, reason about the information it receives, and act autonomously to achieve its goals. Its structure comprises several key components that work together seamlessly to ensure the agent functions effectively in dynamic and complex environments.

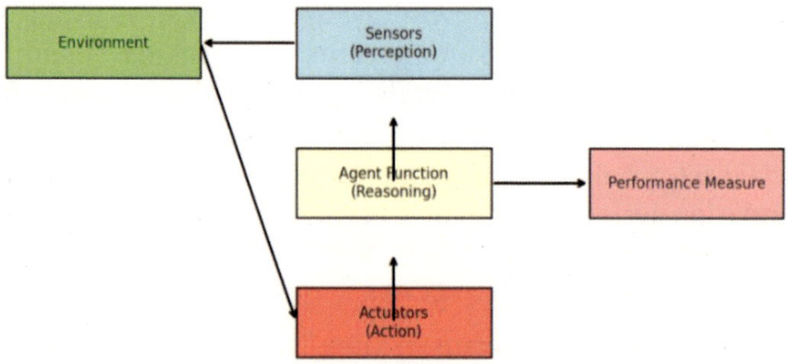

Figure 1.10: Intelligent Agent.

Above Figure 1.10 representing an intelligent agent. It illustrates the interactions between the sensors (perception), agent function (reasoning), actuators (action), the environment, and the performance measure that evaluates the agent's success.

- Below are the main components of an intelligent agent, explained in detail:

1. Environment

The environment is the external context in which the agent operates. It consists of everything the agent interacts with or perceives, including physical objects, other agents, or virtual data sources. Environments can vary widely in nature:

- Fully Observable vs. Partially Observable: In fully observable environments, the agent has complete and accurate information at all times, enabling precise decision-making. In contrast, partially observable environments provide incomplete or uncertain data, requiring the agent to infer missing information.
- Static vs. Dynamic: Static environments remain constant unless acted upon, while dynamic environments change over time, requiring the agent to adapt continuously.

For example, an autonomous car operates in a dynamic, partially observable environment that includes other vehicles, traffic signals, pedestrians, and road conditions.

2. Sensors (Perception)

Sensors are the mechanisms through which the agent perceives the environment. These devices or components capture real-time data and convert it into a format the agent can process. Sensors are essential for understanding the current state of the environment and play a critical role in the decision-making process.

Examples of sensors include:

- Cameras in self-driving cars to detect obstacles and traffic signals.
- Microphones in virtual assistants like Alexa or Siri to process voice commands.
- Infrared sensors in robots to measure proximity or heat.

Sensors must be accurate and reliable, as the quality of the data they collect directly affects the agent's performance.

3. Agent Function (Reasoning and Decision-Making)

The agent function is the reasoning component of the intelligent agent. It processes data from the sensors to map perceptions to actions. This component determines the agent's behavior and ensures its actions are aligned with its objectives.

The agent function is responsible for:

- Interpreting Inputs: Understanding and analyzing the current state of the environment.
- Making Decisions: Choosing the most appropriate action based on predefined rules, algorithms, or learned behavior.
- Learning and Adapting: In advanced agents, the reasoning component evolves over time, improving decision-making through experience.

The agent function varies depending on the type of agent. For instance, simple reflex agents rely on predefined rules, while utility-based agents use optimization techniques to maximize desirable outcomes.

4. Actuators (Action)

Actuators enable the agent to execute actions and interact with the environment. These components perform the tasks decided by the agent function, allowing the agent to affect its surroundings. Actuators can be physical or virtual, depending on the application.

Examples include:

- Steering mechanisms and brakes in autonomous vehicles for navigation and control.
- Robotic arms in manufacturing for assembling products.
- Display systems in recommendation engines to show personalized suggestions to users.
- Actuators are critical for bridging the gap between decision-making and real-world action, ensuring the agent can implement its plans effectively.

5. Performance Measure

The performance measure evaluates the success of the agent's actions in achieving its goals. It provides feedback on how effectively the agent performs, enabling continuous improvement. The performance measure is vital for refining the agent's behavior and ensuring it adapts to changing conditions.

Examples of performance measures include:

- In a game-playing agent, winning or achieving a high score serves as the performance measure.
- In a recommendation system, metrics like click-through rates or user engagement evaluate success.
- For an autonomous vehicle, metrics like safety, fuel efficiency, and timely arrival at the destination are used.
- Performance measures ensure the agent remains focused on its objectives and improves over time.

Integration of Components

The structure of an intelligent agent integrates these components into a cohesive system. Sensors collect data from the environment, which is processed by the agent function to decide actions. Actuators execute these decisions, affecting the environment, while the performance measure evaluates the outcomes and feeds back into the agent function for optimization. This feedback loop enables the agent to operate effectively in dynamic and complex scenarios.

Behavior and Task Environment

Understanding Behavior

In artificial intelligence (AI), behavior refers to the observable actions or responses of an intelligent agent as it interacts with its environment. Behavior is determined by the agent's design, its understanding of the environment, and its reasoning process. The quality of an agent's behavior is evaluated based on its ability to achieve predefined goals while adapting to the constraints and dynamics of the environment. For example, the behavior of a self-driving car includes decisions like lane changes, braking, or acceleration, all aligned with the goal of safe and efficient navigation. An agent's behavior is influenced by its perceptual capabilities (how well it understands the environment), its internal logic (decision-making algorithms), and its ability to execute actions (actuators). Effective behavior requires not just responding to immediate stimuli but also anticipating future events and adjusting actions accordingly. Intelligent agents are designed to exhibit rational behavior, meaning they act in ways that maximize their chances of achieving specific objectives.

Task Environment

The task environment is the external context within which an intelligent agent operates. It defines the scope, rules, constraints, and conditions that shape the agent's actions and decisions. A task environment includes everything the agent interacts with, including physical objects, other agents, and virtual systems. For instance, in a warehouse, the task environment of a robotic agent might include shelves, goods, human workers, and the layout of the space.

Task environments can vary based on several characteristics:

- Fully Observable vs. Partially Observable: A fully observable environment provides the agent with complete information at all times. In contrast, a partially observable environment offers incomplete or noisy data, requiring the agent to infer missing information.
- Static vs. Dynamic: In a static environment, the conditions remain constant unless altered by the agent. Dynamic environments change over time, often independently of the agent's actions.

- Deterministic vs. Stochastic: Deterministic environments produce predictable outcomes for actions, while stochastic environments involve uncertainty in outcomes.

Interaction Between Behavior and Task Environment

The task environment directly influences an agent's behavior. To succeed, the agent must adapt its actions to fit the specific nature of the environment.

For example:

- In a deterministic and static environment, an agent can rely on predefined rules to achieve its goals.
- In a dynamic and stochastic environment, the agent must continuously learn, adapt, and make probabilistic decisions to handle uncertainty.

An agent's behavior can also modify the task environment. For instance, a cleaning robot might rearrange objects while performing its tasks, altering its surroundings in the process. This interplay between behavior and environment forms a feedback loop, where the environment shapes the agent's actions, and the agent's actions influence the environment.

Examples and Applications

The relationship between behavior and task environment can be seen in various AI applications:

- Autonomous Vehicles: The task environment includes roads, traffic, and weather conditions, influencing the vehicle's behavior, such as speed control or lane changes.
- Robotics: In manufacturing, robots adapt their behavior to the layout of the workspace and the position of tools or materials.
- Gaming AI: The task environment includes the rules of the game and player actions, shaping the AI's strategies and moves.

By designing agents that align their behavior with the demands of the task environment, AI systems can achieve higher levels of efficiency, adaptability, and effectiveness. Understanding and addressing this relationship is a critical aspect of creating intelligent, goal-oriented agents.

Conclusion

Chapter 1 introduces the fundamental concepts of Artificial Intelligence (AI), tracing its evolution, applications, and goals. It explains key ideas like the Turing Test, which evaluates a machine's ability to exhibit intelligent behavior indistinguishable from humans. The distinctions between Weak AI, Strong AI, and Narrow AI are explored, alongside ambitious pursuits of Artificial General Intelligence (AGI) and Super AI, which aim to surpass human cognitive abilities.

The chapter also discusses the Rational Agent Approach, focusing on designing agents that act logically to achieve predefined objectives. Further, the chapter delves into the structure of intelligent agents, highlighting components like sensors, actuators, and reasoning mechanisms, and their interaction with dynamic task environments. Lastly, it examines the importance of adaptive behavior and the interplay between an agent's actions and its environment. Next Chapter explores the essential techniques for problem-solving and search in AI, starting with problem characteristics, production systems, and control strategies. It covers foundational algorithms like Breadth-First Search and Depth-First Search, advanced methods such as Hill Climbing, Best-First Search, and the A Algorithm*, and delves into solving Constraint Satisfaction Problems and Means-End Analysis. The chapter concludes with game-playing strategies, including the Min-Max Algorithm and Alpha-Beta Pruning, offering insights into AI decision-making and strategic reasoning.

Exercise:

- Define Artificial Intelligence and explain its key goals and objectives.
- What is the Turing Test, and how does it evaluate machine intelligence?
- Differentiate between Weak AI, Strong AI, and Narrow AI with examples.
- Explain Artificial General Intelligence (AGI) and Super AI. How are they different from Narrow AI?
- Describe the Rational Agent Approach in AI. What are its main principles?
- Outline the structure of an intelligent agent. Explain the role of sensors and actuators.
- What is the significance of behavior in intelligent agents? Provide an example.
- Discuss the characteristics of task environments. How do they influence an agent's behavior?
- Compare and contrast Fully Observable and Partially Observable environments with examples.

Explain how the interaction between an agent's behavior and its task environment creates a feedback loop. Provide a real-world example.

2

Problem Solving and Searching Techniques

Introduction

This chapter focuses on problem-solving and search techniques in AI, providing a foundation for tackling complex tasks systematically. It covers problem characteristics, production systems, and control strategies, along with essential algorithms like Breadth-First Search, Depth-First Search, Hill Climbing, heuristic searches, and game-playing strategies such as Min-Max and Alpha-Beta Pruning.

Objective

The objective of this chapter is to introduce various problem-solving and search techniques used in AI, ranging from fundamental algorithms to advanced strategies. It aims to equip readers with the knowledge to model problems, apply efficient search methods, and understand strategic decision-making in diverse domains.

Problem Characteristics

In Artificial Intelligence (AI), understanding the characteristics of a problem is crucial for selecting the appropriate algorithm or methodology to solve it. Problems can differ significantly in their structure, complexity, and requirements, and these variations influence how they are approached and solved by AI systems.

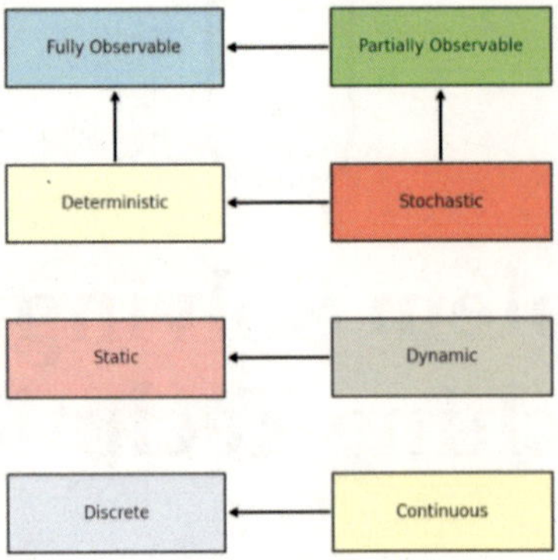

Figure 2.1: Problem Attributes Vary in AI Environments.

Figure 2.1 illustrates important aspects such as "Fully Observable vs. Partially Observable," "Deterministic vs. Stochastic," and others. The diagram highlights the differences and provides a clear understanding of how problem attributes vary in AI environments.

Table 2.1 summarizing the problem characteristics:

Table 2.1: Problem Characteristics.

Problem Characteristic	Description	Example
Fully Observable vs. Partially Observable	Specifies whether the agent has complete or partial information about the environment.	Chess (Fully Observable), Poker (Partially Observable)
Deterministic vs. Stochastic	Defines if outcomes are predictable or involve uncertainty due to randomness.	Maze Solving (Deterministic), Weather Forecasting (Stochastic)
Static vs. Dynamic	Indicates whether the environment changes independently of the agent's actions.	Sudoku (Static), Driving in Traffic (Dynamic)
Discrete vs. Continuous	Distinguishes between finite states/ actions and continuous variables.	Solving Sudoku (Discrete), Robotic Arm Control (Continuous)
Single-Agent vs. Multi-Agent	Determines if the problem involves one agent or multiple interacting agents.	Warehouse Robot (Single-Agent), Soccer Game AI (Multi-Agent)
Episodic vs. Sequential	Classifies tasks as either independent (episodic) or interdependent (sequential).	Image Classification (Episodic), Chess (Sequential)
Known vs. Unknown	States whether the rules and state transitions are predefined or must be learned.	Board Games (Known), Autonomous Navigation in Unknown Terrain (Unknown)

Below are the primary characteristics of problems that are considered when designing AI solutions:

1. Fully Observable vs. Partially Observable

In fully observable problems, the agent has complete information about the state of the environment at any given time. This allows the agent to make precise decisions without uncertainty. For example, in the game of chess, all pieces and their positions are visible to both players, enabling the agent to calculate the best move with full knowledge of the state. Fully observable problems are generally easier to solve because there is no need to infer missing information or handle ambiguities.On the other hand, partially observable problems provide only incomplete or noisy data about the environment. In such cases, the agent must infer missing information to make decisions. For instance, in poker, players can only see their own cards and must deduce the likely hands of opponents based on observed actions. Addressing partial observability requires probabilistic reasoning techniques such as Bayesian networks or partially observable Markov decision processes (POMDPs), which allow the agent to model and infer hidden states.

2. Deterministic vs. Stochastic

Deterministic problems are those where the outcome of every action is predictable and not influenced by randomness. For example, solving a mathematical equation is a deterministic problem since the solution is fixed and follows predefined rules. These problems can often be tackled using deterministic algorithms such as backtracking or exhaustive search, as there are no uncertainties to account for.In contrast, stochastic problems involve uncertainty, where actions may lead to different outcomes depending on probabilistic factors. Weather prediction, for instance, is a stochastic problem as it involves many unpredictable variables, such as atmospheric conditions and temperature changes. Solving stochastic problems requires methods like Monte Carlo simulations, probabilistic models, or reinforcement learning, which are equipped to handle randomness and make decisions under uncertainty.

3. Static vs. Dynamic

Static problems involve environments that remain constant while the agent is deliberating or acting. In these scenarios, the agent can plan its actions in advance without worrying about unexpected changes in the environment. For example, solving a crossword puzzle is a static problem since the layout of the grid and clues do not change during the process.Dynamic problems, on the other hand, involve environments that evolve over time, often independently of the agent's actions. For instance, driving a car in traffic is a dynamic problem, as the environment changes continuously due to the movements of other vehicles, pedestrians, and traffic signals. Agents tackling dynamic problems must rely on real-time decision-making techniques and adaptive algorithms, such as reinforcement learning or online planning, to respond effectively to changing conditions.

4. Discrete vs. Continuous

Discrete problems involve a finite number of states, actions, or events, making them easier to model and solve. An example of a discrete problem is Sudoku, where the grid, numbers, and rules are clearly defined and finite. Discrete problems are often solved using search algorithms like depth-first or breadth-first search, which systematically explore the state space. Continuous problems, in contrast, involve infinite or uncountable states and actions, requiring more complex solutions. For example, controlling a robotic arm involves continuous variables such as joint angles and velocities. These problems demand advanced mathematical and computational techniques like gradient descent, optimization methods, or control theory to manage the continuous nature of the variables.

5. Single-Agent vs. Multi-Agent

In single-agent problems, only one decision-making entity is involved, simplifying the problem since the agent does not need to account for interactions with others. For example, solving a maze involves only one agent navigating through a fixed environment to reach its goal. Single-agent problems are often tackled using search-based methods or heuristic algorithms that focus solely on optimizing the agent's performance.

Multi-agent problems involve multiple entities that may cooperate, compete, or act independently. For instance, online multiplayer games feature multiple players, each with their own objectives. In such scenarios, the agents' decisions are influenced by the actions of others, requiring approaches like game theory, multi-agent reinforcement learning, or negotiation strategies. The complexity of multi-agent problems lies in predicting and adapting to the behavior of other agents.

6. Episodic vs. Sequential

Episodic problems consist of independent decisions or actions, where the outcome of one decision does not affect the next. For example, classifying images in a dataset is an episodic problem because each classification task is unrelated to the others. Episodic problems are often addressed using machine learning models, such as supervised learning, where the agent focuses solely on the current task. Sequential problems, on the other hand, involve interdependent actions, where the outcome of one decision influences future states and decisions. Chess is a classic example of a sequential problem, where each move affects the progression of the game and the available options in subsequent turns. Solving sequential problems requires techniques like dynamic programming, Markov decision processes (MDPs), or reinforcement learning to plan and optimize long-term strategies.

7. Known vs. Unknown

In known problems, the rules, states, and outcomes are well-defined and understood. This allows the agent to plan its actions with precision, leveraging predefined models or algorithms. For example, solving a mathematical optimization problem involves known variables, constraints, and objectives, enabling the use of deterministic methods. Unknown problems, however, require the agent to learn or explore the environment to understand its rules and states. For instance, navigating an unfamiliar city involves an unknown environment, where the agent must explore routes and landmarks to reach its destination. Addressing unknown problems often involves reinforcement learning, where the agent learns optimal behaviors through trial and error, or exploratory algorithms that gather information about the environment.

Production Systems

A production system is a fundamental architecture used in artificial intelligence (AI) for problem-solving and decision-making. It operates using a set of rules, known as productions, and a working memory that holds the current state of the system. Production systems are designed to model intelligent behavior by breaking down problems into smaller, manageable rules and systematically applying them to reach a goal (Figure 2.2).

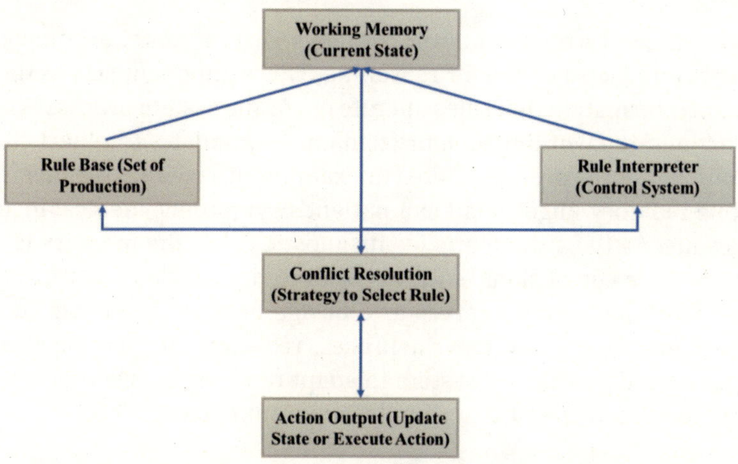

Figure 2.2: Representing the Flow of Production Systems.

Components of a Production System

A production system operates based on four primary components: Set of Rules, Working Memory, Rule Interpreter, and Conflict Resolution Mechanism. These components work together to process information, apply logical reasoning, and execute actions to achieve predefined goals. Below is a detailed explanation of each component:

1. Set of Rules (Productions)

The set of rules forms the core of a production system. These rules are expressed in the form of if-then statements that specify the conditions under which certain actions should be taken. Each rule has two parts:

- Condition (If): Describes the scenario or criteria that must be met.
- Action (Then): Specifies the operation or response to be performed when the condition is satisfied.

These rules allow the system to break down complex tasks into smaller, manageable steps. For instance, in a traffic light control system, a rule might state:

IF traffic is heavy THEN extend green light duration. This ensures that the traffic flow adapts dynamically to the number of vehicles. Rules are modular, meaning new ones can be added without significantly altering the system, making production systems highly flexible.

The effectiveness of a production system heavily depends on the comprehensiveness and accuracy of its rules. Poorly defined or incomplete rules can lead to incorrect or suboptimal decisions. Hence, rule design and validation are critical for ensuring the system's reliability.

2. Working Memory

Working memory represents the system's current state, encompassing all relevant data and facts needed for reasoning. This component acts as the central repository of information that rules operate on. As the system processes rules and executes actions, the working memory dynamically updates to reflect changes in the environment or the problem state.For example, in a medical diagnosis system, the working memory might include a patient's symptoms, medical history, and lab test results. As the system applies diagnostic rules, the memory is updated with intermediate conclusions, such as suspected conditions or recommended treatments.Working memory serves as a bridge between the environment and the rule base, ensuring the system can process real-time information. Its dynamic nature enables the production system to adapt to changing scenarios, making it suitable for tasks in dynamic and complex environments.

3. Rule Interpreter (Control System)

The rule interpreter is responsible for identifying and applying the appropriate rules from the set of rules based on the current state in the working memory. This component matches the conditions specified in the rules against the data in the working memory to determine which rules are applicable at a given time.If multiple rules match the current state, the rule interpreter must defer to the conflict resolution mechanism to select one. For example, in a medical diagnosis system, if multiple diagnostic rules apply to a patient's symptoms, the interpreter delegates the decision to the conflict resolution mechanism.The rule interpreter ensures that the production system functions systematically by controlling the flow of reasoning. It also facilitates modularity, as the interpreter can handle changes to the rule base or working memory without requiring significant modifications to the system's architecture.

4. Conflict Resolution Mechanism

When multiple rules are applicable to the current state, the conflict resolution mechanism resolves ambiguities by selecting the most appropriate rule to execute. This component is critical for ensuring that the system makes logical and effective decisions, especially in scenarios with overlapping or conflicting rules.

Common conflict resolution strategies include:

- Specificity: Prefer rules with more specific conditions, as they are tailored to address particular scenarios.
- Recency: Prioritize rules based on the most recently updated data in the working memory, ensuring decisions are based on the latest information.
- Priority: Assign fixed priorities to rules and select the highest-priority rule when conflicts arise.

For instance, in a traffic light system, rules for handling emergency vehicles might be given higher priority than rules for regular traffic. This ensures that emergency situations are addressed promptly without disrupting the overall traffic flow.

The conflict resolution mechanism ensures the system remains efficient and consistent, preventing unnecessary delays or errors caused by indecision. Its design significantly influences the performance and reliability of the production system.

Working of a Production System

The operation of a production system follows a systematic process involving initialization, rule matching, conflict resolution, rule execution, and termination. These steps enable the system to process information, apply logic, and execute actions to solve problems or make decisions. Below Figure 2.3 is a detailed explanation of each step:

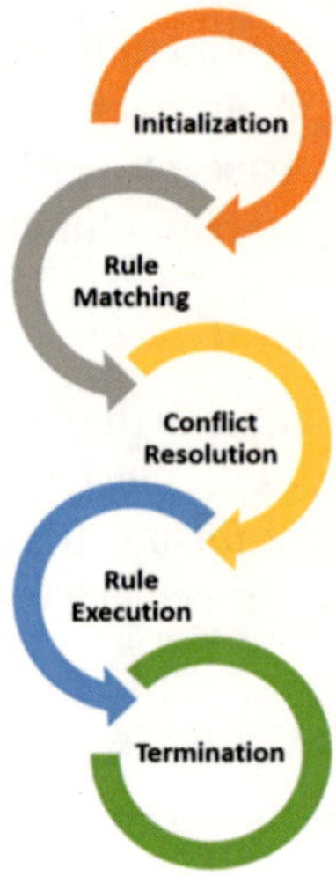

Figure 2.3: Steps.

Initialization

The working memory of the production system is initialized with an initial set of data or facts. This represents the starting point for the system's reasoning process. Initialization is crucial as it provides the context or problem state that the system will operate on. For example, in a game-playing agent like chess, the initial state of the working memory might include the positions of all the pieces on the board. In a diagnostic system, the initial data could include a patient's symptoms and medical history. Proper initialization ensures that the system begins with accurate and relevant information, laying the foundation for effective decision-making.

Rule Matching

In this step, the rule interpreter examines the conditions of each rule in the rule base and matches them against the current state of the working memory. The goal is to identify all the rules whose conditions are satisfied by the data in the working memory. This process involves comparing the "if" conditions of rules to the available facts. Multiple rules may match simultaneously, creating a situation where more than one rule could potentially be applied. For instance, in a robotic navigation system, two rules might match: one directing the robot to move forward if the path is clear and another directing it to turn if an obstacle is detected. Rule matching is essential for identifying all possible actions the system can take in a given state.

Conflict Resolution

When multiple rules match the current state, the conflict resolution mechanism selects the most appropriate rule to fire. This step ensures that the system avoids ambiguity and executes only one action at a time. Conflict resolution uses predefined strategies to determine the rule to be applied:

- Specificity: Prefer the rule with the most specific conditions, as it is more likely to address the situation precisely.
- Recency: Choose the rule based on the most recently updated data in the working memory.
- Priority: Select the rule with the highest priority, as defined in the system's configuration.

For example, in a traffic control system, a rule for handling emergency vehicles might override a general rule for managing regular traffic. Conflict resolution ensures that the system acts logically and efficiently in situations with overlapping or competing rules.

Rule Execution

Once a rule is selected, it is fired, and the specified action is executed. This leads to a change in the working memory or an interaction with the external environment.

For example:

- In a chess-playing system, executing a rule might involve updating the position of a chess piece on the board.
- In a medical diagnosis system, it might involve adding a suspected diagnosis to the working memory or recommending a specific test.

Rule execution is critical as it drives the system towards achieving its goal by applying logical actions based on the current state. After execution, the working memory is updated to reflect the changes, setting the stage for the next cycle of reasoning.

Termination

The system continues the cycle of rule matching, conflict resolution, and rule execution until a termination condition is met. Termination conditions vary depending on the application:

- Achieving the Goal: The system stops once the desired objective is achieved, such as solving a puzzle or diagnosing a condition.
- Exhausting Rules: The system halts when no more applicable rules are available for the current state.
- Time or Resource Limits: The system may stop if predefined limits on time or computational resources are reached.

For instance, in a chess game, the system may terminate after achieving a checkmate or when no valid moves are left. Proper termination criteria ensure that the system does not enter infinite loops and remains efficient.

Types of Production Systems

1. Monotonic Production Systems

Monotonic production systems are characterized by the property that once a rule is applied, it cannot be undone. This means that the system's working memory only expands with new information and never retracts or revises previously applied rules. Monotonic systems are particularly suited for problems where actions are irreversible, such as mathematical proofs or logical deductions. In such systems, applying rules step-by-step ensures progress toward the solution without backtracking. For example, in a mathematical proof, once a theorem is proven using specific axioms or rules, it becomes a permanent part of the reasoning process. This simplifies the system's operation and ensures consistency but limits flexibility in dynamic environments where facts might change.

2. Non-Monotonic Production Systems

Non-monotonic production systems allow for revisions in conclusions when new information becomes available. Unlike monotonic systems, these systems can retract previous conclusions if they are contradicted by updated data. This feature makes non-monotonic systems suitable for dynamic environments where the state of knowledge evolves over time. An example is weather forecasting. Initial predictions based on early data might be revised as new weather patterns emerge. Non-monotonic systems are vital for handling uncertainty and adapting to changes, but they require more complex mechanisms to manage the retraction and re-evaluation of rules.

3. Partially Commutative Production Systems

In partially commutative production systems, the order in which rules are applied does not affect the final outcome, provided that all applicable rules are eventually executed. This ensures consistency in the results, regardless of the sequence of rule execution. These systems are often used for problems with well-defined mathematical properties. For example, in arithmetic calculations, the order of addition operations does not affect the final sum (e.g., 3+4+5=4+5+3). Partially commutative systems offer flexibility in rule execution while ensuring predictable outcomes, making them efficient for certain types of problem-solving.

4. Commutative Production Systems

Commutative production systems guarantee the same results regardless of the sequence of rule applications. They extend the concept of partial commutativity by ensuring that all permutations of rule applications lead to identical outcomes. These systems are often used in applications where consistency and reliability are critical. For instance, sorting algorithms, such as bubble sort or quicksort, ensure that the final output—a sorted list—is always the same, no matter the sequence of intermediate steps. Commutative systems are particularly useful in ensuring reproducibility and correctness in deterministic tasks.

Applications of Production Systems

Expert Systems: Production systems are widely used in expert systems for diagnostic and advisory tasks. These systems rely on a set of rules to analyze data and provide recommendations. For example, MYCIN, an early medical diagnosis system, uses production rules to recommend treatments based on patient symptoms, while DENDRAL helps chemists analyze molecular structures. Expert systems demonstrate the power of production systems in handling specialized knowledge and reasoning tasks.

Natural Language Processing (NLP): In natural language processing, grammar rules can be represented as production rules to parse and understand language. For instance, a rule might specify that a sentence consists of a noun phrase followed by a verb phrase. By applying such rules iteratively, a production system can analyze and generate syntactically correct sentences. This application showcases the utility of production systems in breaking down complex linguistic structures into manageable components.

Game AI: Production systems are integral to game AI, where they help decision-making in strategy games like chess, checkers, and Go. These systems analyze the current game state and apply rules to determine optimal moves. For example, a rule in chess might state: "If the opponent's king is exposed, THEN move the queen to check." Production systems in game AI exemplify their ability to process large rule sets and adapt to dynamic scenarios.

Industrial Automation: In manufacturing, production systems guide robotic arms and assembly lines by applying rules that control actions like picking, placing, and assembling components. For example, a rule might state: "IF a defect is detected, THEN remove the item from the line." These systems enhance efficiency and precision in industrial processes, making them a cornerstone of automation.

Problem Solving: Production systems are also employed in general problem-solving tasks, such as pathfinding, planning, and decision support systems. For instance, in a navigation system, a rule might state: "IF the current route is blocked, THEN find an alternate route." These systems excel in domains where structured reasoning is required to achieve specific goals.

Advantages of Production Systems

1. Modularity

Production systems are highly modular, as rules can be added, removed, or modified independently without disrupting the entire system. This feature makes them flexible and easy to maintain, especially in complex domains. For example, in a diagnostic system, new medical conditions can be incorporated by simply adding relevant rules without reconfiguring the entire system.

2. Transparency

Each rule in a production system is interpretable, making the reasoning process transparent and easy to debug. This helps developers understand why a particular action was taken or why a specific conclusion was reached. For instance, in expert systems, transparency ensures that medical professionals can trust the recommendations provided by the system.

3. Flexibility

Production systems are versatile and can be applied to both static environments, such as mathematical problem-solving, and dynamic systems, such as traffic management. Their adaptability to various applications makes them a powerful tool in AI.

4. Scalability

Production systems can scale to accommodate larger problem domains by adding new rules. For instance, a traffic control system can expand to manage additional intersections by introducing rules for each new scenario. This scalability makes production systems ideal for evolving applications.

Limitations of Production Systems

- Conflict Resolution Overhead: When multiple rules apply, resolving conflicts can become computationally expensive, especially in systems with large rule sets. This overhead can slow down decision-making and reduce efficiency in real-time applications.
- Limited Learning Capability: Most production systems do not inherently learn or adapt to new scenarios. Instead, they rely on predefined rules, which require external modification to address new problems. This limitation reduces their effectiveness in dynamic or unpredictable environments.
- Rule Explosion: As problems grow in complexity, the number of rules required can increase exponentially, leading to a phenomenon known as rule explosion. Managing and maintaining such extensive rule sets can be challenging and error-prone.
- Dependency on Rule Quality: The performance of a production system depends heavily on the accuracy and completeness of its rules. Poorly designed or incomplete rules can lead to incorrect or suboptimal decisions, undermining the system's reliability and effectiveness.

Control Strategies

In the realm of Artificial Intelligence (AI), particularly within production systems, control strategies are pivotal in guiding the application of rules to efficiently navigate from an initial state to a desired goal state. These strategies ensure that AI systems operate effectively, making informed decisions while optimizing computational resources.

Let's explore deeper into the important aspects of control strategies:

Rule Selection

Rule selection is the process by which a production system determines which rule to apply when multiple rules are applicable to the current state. This decision-making is crucial, as the chosen rule influences the system's subsequent actions and overall trajectory toward the goal. Effective rule selection involves evaluating the conditions of applicable rules and selecting the one that best aligns with the system's objectives. For instance, in an expert system designed for medical diagnosis, if multiple diagnostic rules match a patient's symptoms, the system must decide which rule to apply first. This decision could be based on factors such as the specificity of the rule, the severity of the condition it addresses, or the reliability of the information it provides. Implementing efficient rule selection mechanisms enhances the system's performance by ensuring that the most relevant and effective rules are applied promptly. This not only accelerates problem-solving but also improves the accuracy and reliability of the AI system's outputs.

Conflict Resolution

In scenarios where multiple rules are simultaneously applicable, a conflict resolution strategy is employed to determine which rule should take precedence. This is essential to prevent ambiguity and ensure a clear, deterministic course of action.

Several strategies are commonly used for conflict resolution:

- Specificity: Preferring rules with more specific conditions, as they are tailored to address particular scenarios.
- Recency: Choosing rules based on the most recently updated information in the working memory, ensuring decisions are based on the latest data.
- Priority: Assigning fixed priorities to rules and selecting the highest-priority one when conflicts arise.

For example, in a traffic control system, rules for handling emergency vehicles might be given higher priority than those for regular traffic, ensuring that critical situations are addressed promptly. Effective conflict resolution mechanisms are vital for maintaining the efficiency and consistency of production systems, preventing unnecessary delays or errors caused by indecision.

Search Control

Search control refers to the methods employed to navigate through the problem space efficiently, guiding the system toward the goal state while minimizing computational effort. This involves determining the sequence in which states are explored and ensuring that the search process is both effective and resource-efficient.

Common search control strategies include:

- Depth-First Search (DFS): Explores as far down a branch as possible before backtracking, which can be memory-efficient but may get trapped in deep, unproductive paths.
- Breadth-First Search (BFS): Explores all nodes at the present depth level before moving on to nodes at the next depth level, ensuring the shortest path is found but potentially requiring more memory.
- Heuristic Search: Utilizes domain-specific knowledge to estimate the most promising path to the goal, improving efficiency by prioritizing certain paths over others.

For instance, in a navigation system, heuristic search algorithms like A* can be used to find the shortest route by estimating distances to the destination, thereby reducing the search space and improving response times. Implementing effective search control strategies is crucial for optimizing the performance of AI systems, enabling them to solve complex problems within reasonable time frames and resource constraints.

Efficiency and Resource Management

Control strategies play a pivotal role in enhancing the efficiency of AI systems by ensuring that computational resources are utilized optimally. By guiding the selection and application of rules, these strategies help in reducing unnecessary computations, thereby speeding up the problem-solving process.

Effective resource management involves:

- Avoiding Redundancy: Preventing the re-evaluation of the same conditions or the re-application of the same rules, which conserves processing power and time.
- Preventing Infinite Loops: Ensuring that the system does not get stuck in cycles by applying the same set of rules repeatedly without making progress toward the goal.
- Memory Management: Efficiently handling the working memory to store only relevant information, thereby reducing the system's memory footprint.

For example, in a real-time monitoring system, control strategies ensure that the system responds to critical alerts promptly without being bogged down by less important data, thereby maintaining high performance and reliability. By managing resources effectively, control strategies enable AI systems to operate within practical constraints, making them viable for real-world applications.

Scalability and Adaptability

Well-designed control strategies contribute significantly to the scalability and adaptability of AI systems. Scalability refers to the system's ability to handle increasing amounts of work or to be expanded to accommodate growth, while adaptability pertains to the system's capacity to adjust to new conditions or modifications in the environment.

Control strategies facilitate scalability by:

- Modularity: Allowing new rules to be added without disrupting existing functionalities, enabling the system to expand its knowledge base as needed.
- Efficient Resource Allocation: Ensuring that as the system grows, resources are allocated in a manner that maintains performance levels.

Adaptability is achieved through:

- Dynamic Rule Application: Enabling the system to apply different rules based on changing conditions, allowing it to respond appropriately to new situations.
- Learning Mechanisms: Incorporating feedback to modify control strategies over time, improving decision-making as the system encounters diverse scenarios.

For instance, in an e-commerce recommendation system, control strategies allow the system to scale by adding new product categories and adapt

Breadth-first Search

Breadth-First Search (BFS) is a fundamental graph traversal algorithm used in many areas, such as computer science, artificial intelligence, and network theory. It systematically explores the vertices (or nodes) and edges of a graph to find the shortest path, solve connectivity problems, or search for specific elements. Breadth-First Search (BFS) is a cornerstone algorithm in Artificial Intelligence and graph theory, designed to systematically traverse or search through graphs or tree structures. It explores all nodes at the current depth level before proceeding to nodes at the next level. BFS guarantees finding the shortest path in an unweighted graph, making it invaluable for solving pathfinding, connectivity, and traversal problems.

Figure 2.4: Flowchart for the Breadth-First Search (BFS) Algorithm.

The algorithm operates by starting at a given source node, marking it as visited, and adding it to a queue (Figure 2.4). From this queue, nodes are dequeued one by one, and their unvisited neighbors are discovered, marked as visited, and enqueued. This process continues until all reachable nodes have been processed, ensuring that no node is visited more than once.BFS's primary feature is its level-order exploration, which ensures that nodes closer to the source are visited before nodes farther away. This property is particularly useful in applications such as shortest path calculations in unweighted graphs, level-order traversal of trees, and systematic exploration in AI-based problems like maze solving.

Steps of BFS

- Start at the source node.
- Enqueue the source and mark it as visited.
- While the queue is not empty:
  - Dequeue a node from the front.
  - Process the node (e.g., add it to the result).
  - For each unvisited neighbor:
    - Mark the neighbor as visited.
    - Enqueue the neighbor.
- Repeat until all reachable nodes are visited.

Applications of BFS in AI

- Shortest Path in Unweighted Graphs: BFS ensures minimal steps between nodes.
- Level Order Traversal: Used in trees for hierarchical data processing.
- Maze Solving: Finds paths in grid-based structures.
- Web Crawling: Systematically visits and indexes websites level by level.
- Social Network Analysis: Determines degrees of separation or reachable connections.

Example:

Consider the following simple graph:

```
 1
/\
2 3
| |
4 5
```

Adjacency List Representation:

```
1: [2, 3]
2: [1, 4]
3: [1, 5]
4: [2]
5: [3]
```

BFS Traversal (Starting from Node 1)

Steps:

Start at Node 1:

- Enqueue 1.
- Mark 1 as visited.

Queue: [1]

Dequeue 1:

- Process 1.
- Enqueue its neighbors (2 and 3).
- Mark 2 and 3 as visited.

Queue: [2, 3]

Dequeue 2:

- Process 2.
- Enqueue its neighbor (4).
- Mark 4 as visited.

Queue: [3, 4]

Dequeue 3:

- Process 3.
- Enqueue its neighbor (5).
- Mark 5 as visited.

Queue: [4, 5]

Dequeue 4:

- Process 4.
- No unvisited neighbors.

Queue: [5]

Dequeue 5:

- Process 5.
- No unvisited neighbors.

Queue: []

Queue is Empty:

- Terminate the algorithm.

BFS Output

The order of traversal is:

1 -> 2 -> 3 -> 4 -> 5

This simple example shows how BFS explores all nodes level by level.

Depth-first Search

Traversal Order

DFS explores the graph by going as deep as possible along one branch before backtracking to explore other branches. It begins at a starting node, visits a neighbor, and keeps diving deeper into the graph until it reaches a dead end (a node with no unvisited neighbors). At this point, it backtracks to explore alternative paths. This nature of traversal makes DFS ideal for problems where you need to exhaustively explore a path before considering others. For example, in a tree structure, DFS would visit a node's left child, then the left child of that child, and so on, until it reaches the deepest node. Only then does it backtrack and start exploring the right children. In a graph, this approach is slightly more complex due to the presence of cycles, where nodes may have multiple connections.

Data Structures Used

DFS can be implemented using recursion or an explicit stack. In a recursive implementation, the program's call stack implicitly handles backtracking, making the code concise and easier to understand. However, recursion can lead to stack overflow for very deep graphs. In contrast, the iterative implementation explicitly uses a stack to manage nodes. The stack ensures that the most recently visited node (and its neighbors) is processed next, maintaining the depth-first nature of the traversal. Using an explicit stack can handle large graphs more safely than recursion.

Graph Types Supported

DFS is versatile and can traverse both directed and undirected graphs. In an undirected graph, DFS helps explore connected components, while in directed graphs, it's useful for tasks like cycle detection and topological sorting. DFS can handle weighted and unweighted graphs, but it doesn't directly consider edge weights during traversal. It simply ensures that all nodes are visited, regardless of edge weight. For shortest-path problems in weighted graphs, algorithms like Dijkstra's or Bellman-Ford are more appropriate.

Applications

DFS has a wide range of applications:

- Pathfinding: DFS helps explore all possible paths between nodes, making it useful in puzzles or mazes.
- Topological Sorting: In a Directed Acyclic Graph (DAG), DFS can order nodes in a sequence such that every edge points from an earlier node to a later node, which is crucial in scheduling problems.
- Cycle Detection: DFS can identify cycles in directed or undirected graphs

by keeping track of visited nodes and the recursion stack (in directed graphs).

- Maze Solving: DFS explores paths exhaustively and finds a solution efficiently when the goal node is at greater depths.
- Connected Components: In undirected graphs, DFS can identify clusters of nodes that are connected to each other.

Algorithm (Recursive and Iterative)

In recursive DFS, a function is repeatedly called for each unvisited neighbor, diving deeper into the graph. This makes the implementation clean but limits its applicability for large graphs due to stack size limits. In contrast, the iterative DFS uses an explicit stack, which ensures better control over memory and avoids stack overflow.

The core algorithm for DFS involves:

- Marking a node as visited.
- Exploring its neighbors recursively or by pushing them onto a stack.
- Backtracking when no unvisited neighbors remain.

Advantages

DFS is memory efficient compared to BFS because it doesn't store all nodes at the current depth. Instead, it only maintains the current path in the stack. This makes it suitable for graphs with high branching factors or when paths are long and narrow. Additionally, its simplicity in finding connected components or checking graph properties makes it a fundamental tool.

Disadvantages

DFS doesn't guarantee finding the shortest path in an unweighted graph. Since it prioritizes depth over breadth, it may explore a longer path before finding the destination. Additionally, without proper cycle detection, DFS can enter infinite loops in cyclic graphs, which is why tracking visited nodes is essential.

Example of Depth-First Search (DFS)

Graph Representation

Consider the following graph:

```
   A
  / \
 B   C
/ \   \
D  E   F
```

This graph can be represented as an adjacency list:

A: [B, C]

B: [A, D, E]

C: [A, F]

D: [B]

E: [B]

F: [C]

DFS Traversal

Starting Node: A

- We begin at node A and explore as deeply as possible along each branch before backtracking.
- Step-by-Step Traversal

Start at Node A:

Mark A as visited.

Visit its first neighbor, B.

Visited: A

Stack: B

Move to Node B:

- Mark B as visited.
- Visit its first neighbor, D.

Visited: A, B

Stack: D

Move to Node D:

- Mark D as visited.
- No unvisited neighbors, backtrack to B.

Visited: A, B, D

Stack: B

Back at Node B:

- Visit its next neighbor, E.
- Visited: A, B, D

Stack: E

Move to Node E:

- Mark E as visited.
- No unvisited neighbors, backtrack to B, then to A.

Visited: A, B, D, E

Stack: A

Back at Node A:

- Visit its next neighbor, C.
- Visited: A, B, D, E

Stack: C

Move to Node C:

- Mark C as visited.
- Visit its only neighbor, F.

Visited: A, B, D, E, C

Stack: F

Move to Node F:

- Mark F as visited.
- No unvisited neighbors, backtrack to C, then to A.

Visited: A, B, D, E, C, F

Stack: Empty

Termination:

- All nodes have been visited, and the stack is empty.

DFS Output

The traversal order is:

A -> B -> D -> E -> C -> F

- DFS Prioritizes Depth: DFS goes deep into the graph, visiting all of a node's descendants before moving to its siblings.
- Backtracking: DFS backtracks when a node has no unvisited neighbors.
- Stack Management: The stack maintains the current path and helps backtrack when necessary.

Hill Climbing and its Variations

Hill Climbing is a heuristic search algorithm used for mathematical optimization problems. It belongs to the family of local search algorithms and is often used to find a good solution to problems with a large search space. The core idea is to start with an arbitrary solution and iteratively move to a neighboring solution that improves the objective function until no further improvement is possible.

Hill Climbing Algorithm

Hill Climbing is a heuristic optimization algorithm widely used in artificial intelligence and computational mathematics to solve problems with a large search space. The essence of Hill Climbing lies in iteratively improving an initial solution by moving to a neighboring solution with a better value for the objective function. This process continues until no further improvement is possible. The algorithm gets its name from the metaphor of climbing to the peak of a hill, where the peak represents the optimal solution. It's a local search algorithm, meaning it focuses on improving the current solution without considering the entire search space.

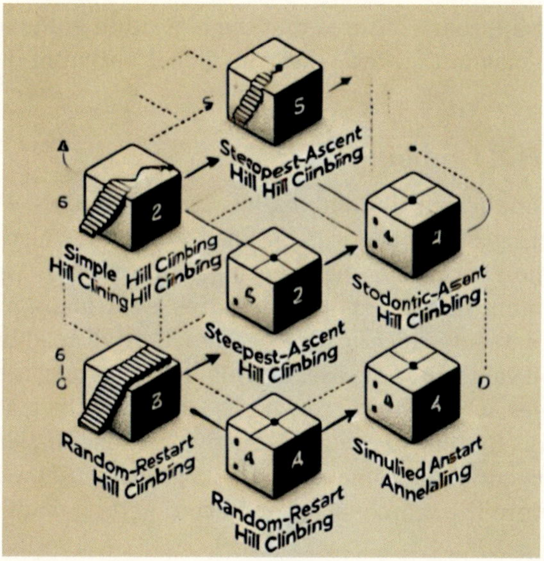

Figure 2.5: Variations of the Hill Climbing Algorithm.

Block diagram representing the variations of the Hill Climbing algorithm in a structured and professional layout, Figure 2.5.

The algorithm begins with a random initial solution and computes the objective function value for that solution. It then generates neighboring solutions by making small adjustments to the current solution. Among these neighbors, it selects the one with the best objective function value and moves to it. If no neighbor offers an improvement, the algorithm terminates. While simple and effective for many problems, Hill Climbing can struggle with local optima, flat plateaus, and ridges, making it a suboptimal choice for certain complex landscapes.

Steps of Hill Climbing

Hill Climbing follows a structured process:

- Start with an Initial Solution: The algorithm begins with a random or predefined starting point in the search space.
- Evaluate the Current Solution: The value of the objective function for the current solution is computed to assess its quality.
- Generate Neighboring Solutions: Small adjustments are made to the current solution to generate neighbors in the search space.
- Move to the Best Neighbor: If a neighboring solution offers an improvement, the algorithm moves to that neighbor and continues.
- Repeat Until Convergence: The process repeats until no better neighbors exist or another termination condition, like a maximum number of iterations, is met.

This iterative approach ensures that the algorithm gradually climbs toward a solution, but it may not always reach the global optimum due to its inherent limitations.

Challenges in Hill Climbing

Despite its simplicity, Hill Climbing has several limitations. One significant challenge is getting stuck in local optima, where the algorithm halts at a suboptimal solution because no neighboring solution offers improvement. This problem is common in complex search spaces with many peaks and valleys. Another issue is plateaus, which are flat regions where all neighbors have the same objective function value. In such cases, the algorithm struggles to make progress. Additionally, ridges, which are narrow paths leading to the global optimum, can be difficult for Hill Climbing to navigate effectively. These challenges highlight the need for variations or enhancements to the basic algorithm, which can improve its ability to explore the search space and avoid getting trapped in suboptimal regions.

Variations of Hill Climbing

To address the limitations of basic Hill Climbing, several variations have been developed:

1. Simple Hill Climbing

Simple Hill Climbing evaluates one neighbor at a time and moves to the first neighbor that improves the solution. This approach is easy to implement but can easily get stuck in local optima or flat plateaus because it doesn't explore multiple neighbors before deciding.

2. Steepest-Ascent Hill Climbing

Steepest-Ascent Hill Climbing improves on the simple approach by evaluating all neighbors and moving to the one that offers the greatest improvement in the objective function. This increases the likelihood of finding better solutions but comes at the cost of additional computation since all neighbors must be evaluated.

3. Stochastic Hill Climbing

In this variation, neighbors are selected randomly, and the algorithm moves to a better solution if it happens to be found. Stochastic Hill Climbing is faster than steepest-ascent and can escape plateaus to some extent, but its random nature may lead to missed opportunities for better solutions.

4. Random-Restart Hill Climbing

This variation involves running the Hill Climbing algorithm multiple times with different random starting points. By restarting from various locations, the algorithm is more likely to escape local optima and find the global optimum. However, it is computationally more expensive as multiple runs are required.

5. Simulated Annealing (a Related Approach)

Simulated Annealing introduces the concept of accepting worse solutions with a certain probability, which decreases over time. This randomness helps the algorithm escape local optima and explore more of the search space, making it particularly effective for complex optimization problems.

Example

To illustrate Hill Climbing, consider finding the maximum value of the function $f(x)=-x2+4x+6$over the range $x\in[0,5]$. The algorithm starts at a random point, say$x=0$, and evaluates the function, $f(0)=6$. It generates neighboring solutions, for example, by incrementing x. Evaluating $f(1)=9$, the algorithm moves to $x=1$. Continuing this process, it finds $f(2)=10$ and moves to $x=2$. At this point, no neighbor improves the value, so the algorithm terminates. The maximum value is $f(2)=10$, reached at $x=2$.

Applications of Hill Climbing

Hill Climbing has diverse applications in artificial intelligence and optimization. In pathfinding, it helps find routes in navigation systems or robotics. In game-playing AI, it evaluates and selects moves based on their potential outcomes. Hill Climbing is also used in operations research for resource allocation, scheduling, and design optimization. Additionally, in machine learning, it assists in tuning hyperparameters to optimize model performance. Hill Climbing is a straightforward and effective algorithm for solving optimization problems, especially when the search space is well-behaved and lacks complex structures. Its variations, such as steepest-ascent, stochastic, and random-restart, address some of its inherent limitations, making it suitable for a broader range of problems. However, understanding its challenges, such as local optima and plateaus, is crucial for choosing the right variation or combining it with other algorithms for better performance (Table 2.2).

Table 2.2: Variations of Hill Climbing Algorithm.

Variation	Description	Pros	Cons
Simple Hill Climbing	Evaluates neighbors one at a time and moves to the first improvement.	Simple to implement and computationally inexpensive.	Prone to getting stuck in local optima or plateaus.
Steepest-Ascent Hill Climbing	Evaluates all neighbors and moves to the one with the greatest improvement.	More likely to find a better solution than Simple Hill Climbing.	Computationally expensive as it evaluates all neighbors.
Stochastic Hill Climbing	Randomly selects a neighbor and moves to it if it improves the solution.	Faster and can escape plateaus to some extent.	Random nature might miss better solutions.
Random-Restart Hill Climbing	Runs the Hill Climbing algorithm multiple times with different starting points.	Increases the chances of finding the global optimum.	Computationally expensive due to multiple restarts.
Simulated Annealing	Allows occasional acceptance of worse solutions to escape local optima.	Effective in escaping local optima and exploring the search space.	Requires careful tuning of the cooling schedule.

Heuristics Search Techniques

Heuristic search techniques are powerful methods used in artificial intelligence to solve complex problems by employing a strategy to make decisions based on estimated solutions. The term "heuristic" refers to a practical approach or rule of thumb that guides the search process, enabling it to find satisfactory solutions efficiently, even in large or complex problem spaces. These techniques are especially useful when exact methods are computationally expensive or infeasible due to the size or nature of the problem. In heuristic search, the algorithm evaluates each state based on a heuristic function, which estimates the "goodness" of that state concerning the goal. This evaluation helps prioritize certain states or paths over others, reducing the number of states the algorithm needs to explore. For example, in a pathfinding problem, a heuristic function might estimate the remaining distance to the goal, guiding the search toward shorter paths.

Flowchart providing an overview of heuristic search techniques (Figure 2.6).

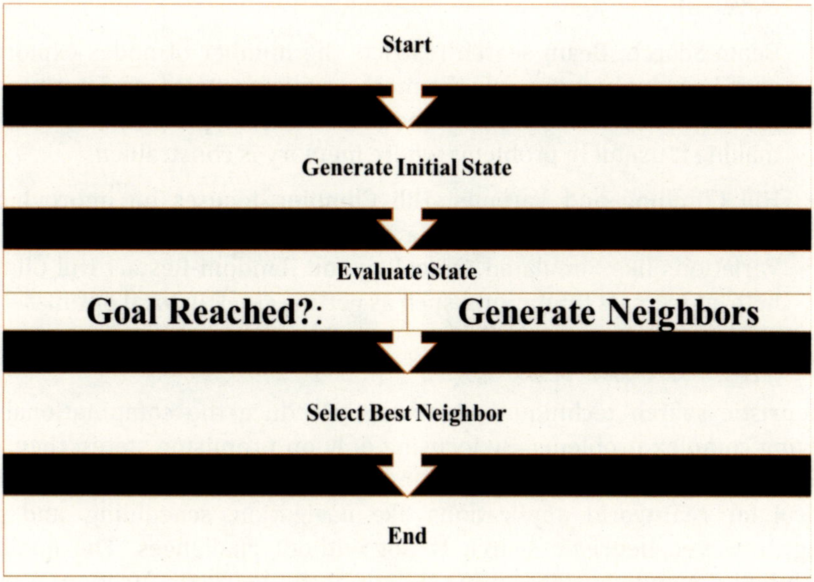

Figure 2.6: Heuristic Search Techniques.

Concepts of Heuristic Search

Heuristic search techniques rely on domain knowledge embedded in the heuristic function, which can vary based on the problem being solved. A well-designed heuristic function significantly improves the algorithm's efficiency by providing good approximations of the solution. However, if the heuristic is poorly chosen or biased, it can lead to suboptimal solutions or inefficient search processes. The effectiveness of heuristic search also depends on the trade-off between exploration (searching new areas of the problem space) and exploitation (focusing on promising areas). Techniques like A* search, Greedy Best-First Search, and Hill Climbing balance this trade-off using heuristics. Heuristic search is particularly valuable in scenarios where the search space is large, such as game-playing AI, robotics, and optimization problems.

Common Heuristic Search Techniques

Greedy Best-First Search: This technique selects the node with the lowest heuristic value at each step, prioritizing states that seem closer to the goal. Although it is efficient and often fast, it does not guarantee finding the optimal solution as it focuses only on the heuristic without considering the cost incurred so far.

- A Search*: A* search combines the heuristic value (estimated cost to the goal) and the cost incurred so far to make decisions. This makes

A* both complete and optimal when the heuristic is admissible (never overestimates the true cost). It is widely used in pathfinding and graph traversal.

- Beam Search: Beam search restricts the number of nodes explored at each level by keeping only the most promising states, as determined by the heuristic function. This method sacrifices completeness for efficiency, making it useful in problems where memory is constrained.
- Hill Climbing and Variants: Hill Climbing focuses on improving the current solution by moving to a neighbor with a better heuristic value. Variations like Simulated Annealing and Random-Restart Hill Climbing help address its limitations, such as getting stuck in local optima.

Advantages and Challenges

Heuristic search techniques significantly reduce the computational cost of solving complex problems. By focusing only on promising states, they avoid unnecessary exploration of large portions of the search space. This makes them practical for real-world applications like navigation, scheduling, and game strategy.However, heuristic search is not without challenges. The quality of the solution depends heavily on the design of the heuristic function. A poorly chosen heuristic can mislead the search, resulting in inefficient exploration or suboptimal solutions. Additionally, heuristic methods are often problem-specific, requiring domain expertise to define effective heuristics.

Applications of Heuristic Search

Heuristic search techniques are extensively used across various domains. In robotics, they enable autonomous robots to navigate complex environments efficiently. In game AI, they guide decision-making processes to compete against human players. Optimization problems, such as scheduling and resource allocation, benefit from heuristic search by finding near-optimal solutions within practical timeframes. Furthermore, heuristic search is crucial in natural language processing and machine learning, where it helps optimize models and find patterns in large datasets. Heuristic search techniques are indispensable tools in artificial intelligence and problem-solving. They balance efficiency and effectiveness, making them suitable for a wide range of applications. While their success depends on the quality of the heuristic, their adaptability and practicality ensure their continued relevance in AI and beyond.

Best-first Search, A* Algorithm

Best-First Search (BFS) is a search algorithm that explores a graph by prioritizing nodes based on a given evaluation function. It combines elements of depth-first and breadth-first search to efficiently find a solution. Best-First Search is heuristic-driven, meaning it uses a heuristic function to estimate the cost or distance to the goal, helping to decide which node to explore next. It is particularly useful for solving pathfinding and graph traversal problems.

Concepts of Best-First Search

- Heuristic Function ($h(n)$: The heuristic function estimates the cost from the current node to the goal node. It determines the order in which nodes are visited.
- Priority Queue: Nodes are stored in a priority queue, sorted by their heuristic values ($h(n)$. The algorithm always expands the node with the smallest $h(n)$ value first.
- Greedy Nature: Best-First Search is also known as Greedy Best-First Search because it prioritizes nodes that appear to be closer to the goal, based on the heuristic.

Steps of Best-First Search

Initialization:

- Start at the initial node and calculate its heuristic value ($h(n)$).
- Insert the initial node into a priority queue.

Node Expansion:

- Remove the node with the smallest $h(n)$) value from the queue.
- If this node is the goal, return the solution.
- Otherwise, generate its neighbors and calculate their heuristic values.

Queue Update:

- Insert the neighbors into the priority queue, maintaining priority based on their heuristic values.

Repeat:

- Continue until the goal is reached or the queue is empty.

Limitations of Best-First Search

- It does not guarantee the shortest path because it only considers the heuristic value ($h(n)$) and ignores the cost to reach the current node ($g(n)$).
- May get stuck in local minima or explore suboptimal paths.

A Algorithm*

The A (A-Star) algorithm* is an extension of Best-First Search that guarantees finding the shortest path if the heuristic function is admissible (never overestimates the true cost). It is widely regarded as one of the most efficient algorithms for pathfinding and graph traversal.

Concepts of A Algorithm*

Evaluation Function:

- f(n)=g(n)+h(n)
- g(n): The cost to reach the current node from the start node.
- h(n): The heuristic cost to reach the goal node from the current node.

Admissible Heuristic:

- A heuristic is admissible if it never overestimates the actual cost to the goal.

Consistency (Monotonicity):

- A heuristic is consistent if, for every node n and successor n', the estimated cost satisfies.

$$h(n) \leq c(n,n')+h(n')$$

where c(n,n′) is the cost of moving from n to n′.

*Steps of A Algorithm**

1. Initialization:

Start at the initial node, calculate f(n)=g(n)+h(n), and insert it into a priority queue.

2. Node Expansion:

- Remove the node with the smallest f(n) value from the queue.
- If this node is the goal, return the solution.
- Otherwise, generate its neighbors.

3. Cost Calculation:

- For each neighbor, calculate:

$$g(n')=g(n)+c(n,n')$$

$$f(n')=g(n')+h(n')')$$

- Insert the neighbor into the priority queue if it hasn't been visited or if the newly calculated f(n′) is smaller.

4. Repeat:

Continue until the goal is reached or the queue is empty

Advantages of A Algorithm*

- Optimality: A* guarantees the shortest path if the heuristic is admissible and consistent.
- Efficiency: A* minimizes the number of nodes expanded by balancing exploration ($g(n)$) and exploitation ($h(n)$).
- Flexibility: A* can adapt to different types of problems by modifying the heuristic function.

Comparison of Best-First Search and An Algorithm as shown in below Table 2.3. Both algorithms are foundational in AI and graph theory, offering unique strengths for various types of search problems. Would you like further clarifications or diagrams?

Table 2.3: Comparison of Best-First Search and A Algorithm*

Feature	Best-First Search	A* Algorithm
Evaluation Function	h(n)h(n)h(n)	f(n)=g(n)+h(n)f(n) = g(n) + h(n) f(n)=g(n)+h(n)
Optimality	Not guaranteed	Guaranteed with admissible heuristic
Efficiency	Fast but may explore suboptimal paths	Balances speed and accuracy effectively
Applications	Pathfinding, approximate solutions	Pathfinding, robotics, and optimal solutions

Constraint Satisfaction Problem

Constraint Satisfaction Problems (CSPs) are a central topic in artificial intelligence and are used to model problems that can be expressed as a set of constraints on variables. CSPs provide a formal framework for solving problems where the goal is to find a solution that satisfies all given constraints. These problems appear in numerous domains, including scheduling, planning, resource allocation, and even puzzles like Sudoku or the N-Queens problem.A CSP is typically represented by a set of variables, each with a domain of possible values, and a set of constraints that specify the allowable combinations of values. The goal is to assign values to all variables such that all constraints are satisfied. For example, in a scheduling problem, the variables might represent time slots, the domains might represent the possible events that can occur in each time slot, and the constraints might ensure that no two events overlap.

Figure 2.7 representing the process of solving a Constraint Satisfaction Problem (CSP):

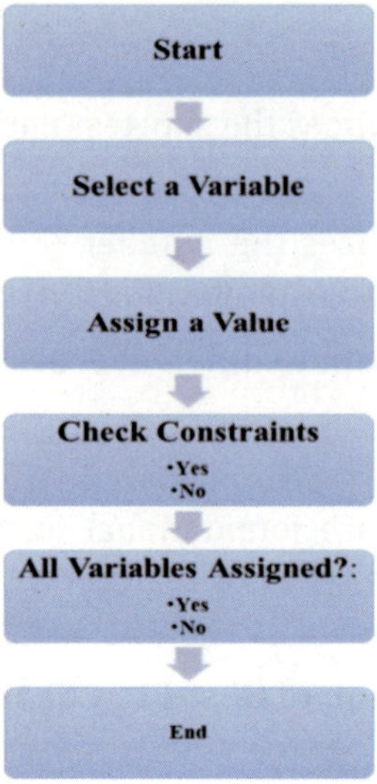

Figure 2.7: process of solving a CSP.

Structure of a CSP

- A CSP can be formally defined as a triplet (X,D,C), where:$X=\{X1,X2,\ldots,Xn\}$ is a set of variables.
- $D=\{D1,D2,\ldots,Dn\}$ is a set of domains, where each domainDi contains the possible values for the corresponding variable,Xi.
- $C=\{C1,C2,\ldots,Ck\}$is a set of constraints, where each constraint specifies the allowable combinations of values for some subset of variables.

For example, consider a graph coloring problem where the goal is to assign colors to nodes such that no two adjacent nodes have the same color. Here, the variables represent the nodes, the domains are the set of available colors, and the constraints ensure that adjacent nodes are not assigned the same color.

Solving CSPs

CSPs are solved by systematically exploring the search space of possible solutions while adhering to the constraints. The most basic method is backtracking, where variables are assigned values sequentially, and if a conflict arises (i.e., a constraint is violated), the algorithm backtracks to try a different assignment. However, naive backtracking can be inefficient, especially for large or complex problems.Advanced techniques like constraint propagation and arc consistency help reduce the search space by eliminating values from variable domains that cannot lead to a valid solution. For example, in the N-Queens problem, placing a queen on the board eliminates rows, columns, and diagonals from consideration for subsequent queens. Techniques like AC-3 (Arc-Consistency Algorithm 3) enforce arc consistency, ensuring that no variable has values in its domain that conflict with constraints on connected variables.To improve efficiency further, heuristics are employed to guide the search. For instance, the minimum remaining values (MRV) heuristic selects the variable with the fewest possible values first, while the degree heuristic prioritizes variables involved in the largest number of constraints. Combining such heuristics with techniques like forward checking creates powerful algorithms that can handle large-scale CSPs effectively.

Applications of CSPs

Constraint Satisfaction Problems are widely applicable in many real-world domains. One prominent application is in scheduling problems, such as assigning employees to shifts or scheduling university courses. In these scenarios, variables represent tasks or time slots, and constraints ensure that resources are not over-allocated or conflicts are avoided. Another application is in resource allocation, where CSPs are used to assign resources like rooms, equipment, or bandwidth to competing tasks under strict constraints.In addition to practical domains, CSPs are used in puzzles and games. For example, solving Sudoku involves assigning numbers to a grid while adhering to constraints that each number appears only once in each row, column, and sub-grid. Similarly, the N-Queens problem challenges us to place N queens on an N×N chessboard without threatening each other. In natural language processing, CSPs are used to model problems like word alignment and syntactic parsing, where constraints help determine the grammatical structure of a sentence.

Challenges and Advancements

While CSPs are powerful, they also pose challenges. The complexity of solving a CSP grows with the number of variables, domains, and constraints, making large-scale CSPs computationally expensive. Handling constraints that involve multiple variables or that are nonlinear adds to the difficulty. Despite these challenges, advancements in algorithms, including local search and hybrid approaches combining CSPs with machine learning, have significantly improved their scalability and applicability.

Local search techniques like min-conflicts iteratively modify an assignment to reduce the number of constraint violations, making them useful for large CSPs. Probabilistic methods and evolutionary algorithms further expand the toolkit for solving CSPs by exploring solutions in non-deterministic ways. These advancements ensure that CSPs remain a cornerstone of AI problem-solving. Constraint Satisfaction Problems provide a robust framework for modeling and solving a wide variety of problems. Their versatility and efficiency, combined with advancements in algorithms, make them indispensable in artificial intelligence and operations research. Whether it's optimizing schedules, solving puzzles, or allocating resources, CSPs continue to play a vital role in finding solutions to complex problems.

Means-end Analysis

Means-End Analysis (MEA) is a heuristic problem-solving technique widely used in artificial intelligence and cognitive science. It involves systematically breaking a problem into smaller, manageable sub-problems by analyzing the difference between the current state and the desired goal state. The central idea of MEA is to minimize this difference iteratively by applying operators—actions that transition the current state toward the goal. MEA is particularly effective in complex problems where direct solutions are not apparent, as it provides a structured approach to achieve incremental progress.In MEA, the problem-solving process begins with defining the initial or current state, the goal state, and the available operators. The algorithm evaluates the difference between the current and goal states, prioritizing the most significant discrepancies. Operators that reduce these differences are selected and applied. If an operator cannot be executed due to unsatisfied preconditions, achieving these preconditions becomes a new sub-goal. This iterative process continues until the current state matches the goal state, ensuring systematic progress (Figure 2.8).

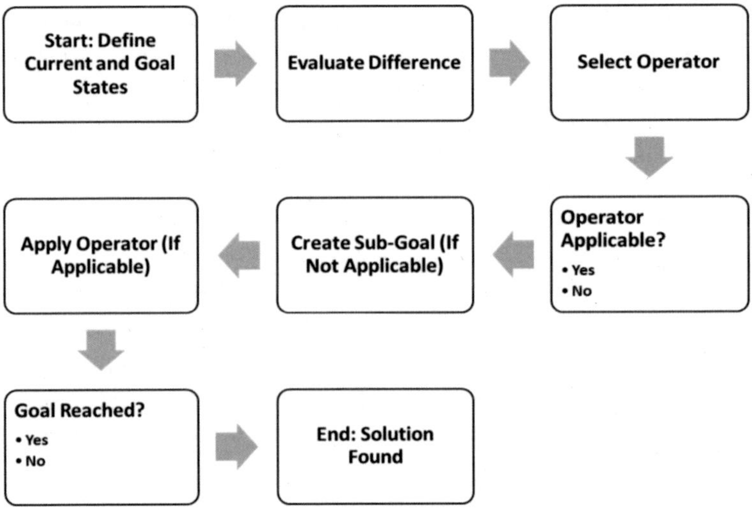

Figure 2.8: Means-End Analysis (MEA) Process.

For example, consider a robot navigating from Room A to Room C, where a locked door separates Room B and Room C. The robot's current state is being in Room A, and the goal state is reaching Room C. The algorithm identifies the locked door as a major difference, selects an operator to move to Room B, and then addresses the sub-goal of unlocking the door. By iteratively applying operators and resolving sub-goals, the robot eventually reaches Room C. This ability to dynamically adapt and resolve intermediate goals showcases the power of MEA in tackling complex problems.MEA is extensively applied in domains like robotics, automated planning, and game AI. In robotics, MEA helps machines determine step-by-step actions to accomplish tasks in dynamic environments. In game AI, characters utilize MEA to navigate challenges by breaking down complex objectives into smaller, actionable goals. Furthermore, MEA is used in educational technologies to create adaptive learning paths for students, helping them progress from their current knowledge level to mastery by addressing intermediate learning goals.

Despite its advantages, MEA has limitations. In problems with vast search spaces or numerous operators, the computational overhead can become significant. Additionally, MEA relies heavily on accurately identifying differences and choosing appropriate operators. If sub-goals conflict or if differences are poorly defined, the problem-solving process can become inefficient or fail entirely. Nonetheless, MEA's structured and goal-driven approach makes it an invaluable technique for solving complex, real-world problems. It continues to play a crucial role in artificial intelligence, offering insights into both machine and human problem-solving strategies.

Introduction to Game Playing

Game playing has been a central area of research in artificial intelligence (AI) since its inception, as it provides a structured environment for studying decision-making and problem-solving. Games are typically well-defined systems with clear rules, a finite set of possible moves, and measurable outcomes, making them an ideal testing ground for AI algorithms. From simple board games like Chess and Checkers to complex multiplayer video games, the principles of game playing in AI can be applied to various domains. In AI, a game is modeledas a search problem where the objective is to find an optimal sequence of moves leading to a desirable outcome. This involves considering all possible moves, predicting the opponent's responses, and evaluating the resulting game states to make decisions. The study of game playing in AI is not limited to recreational purposes; the techniques developed have found applications in real-world problems, such as strategic planning, resource allocation, and automated negotiation systems.

Components of Game Playing in AI

Players: Games involve one or more players. In the context of AI, these can be human players, AI agents, or a combination of both. AI agents aim to simulate intelligent decision-making by considering the game's rules and objectives.

- Game States: A game state represents the current configuration of the game. For example, in Chess, a game state would describe the positions of all pieces on the board at a given time.

- Actions (Moves): Each player can perform specific actions or moves to transition from one game state to another. The set of all possible actions defines the game's dynamics.
- Rules: Rules govern the permissible actions and their effects on the game state. They ensure that the game proceeds in a structured and fair manner.
- Evaluation Function: In many AI game-playing systems, an evaluation function is used to assess the quality of a game state. For example, in Chess, an evaluation function might calculate the relative strength of a player's position based on material advantage and positional factors.
- Objectives: Each player has a specific goal, such as maximizing their score, winning the game, or minimizing the opponent's chances of success. These objectives guide decision-making.

Types of Games in AI

Games can be classified based on certain characteristics:

Deterministic vs. Stochastic:

- Deterministic Games: Games like Chess and Tic-Tac-Toe have no element of chance; outcomes are entirely determined by the players' actions.
- Stochastic Games: Games like Backgammon involve randomness, such as dice rolls, which influence outcomes.

Perfect vs. Imperfect Information:

- Perfect Information Games: All players have complete knowledge of the game state, as in Chess.
- Imperfect Information Games: Players do not have full knowledge of the game state, as in Poker, where opponents' cards are hidden.

Single-Agent vs. Multi-Agent:

- Single-Agent: These are puzzles or games played by one player, such as Sudoku.
- Multi-Agent: These involve interactions between multiple players, such as Chess or Monopoly.

Zero-Sum vs. Non-Zero-Sum:

- Zero-Sum Games: One player's gain is another's loss, as in Checkers or Chess.
- Non-Zero-Sum Games: Players may cooperate to achieve mutual benefits, as in cooperative board games.

AI Techniques in Game Playing

AI employs a range of sophisticated techniques to play games effectively, leveraging the structured nature of games to model them as computational problems. One foundational approach is through search algorithms, where games are treated as search problems involving a game tree that represents all possible moves and their outcomes. Techniques like minimax are used to evaluate the best move by considering the worst possible response from the opponent, ensuring robust decision-making. To enhance efficiency, alpha-beta pruning reduces the number of nodes explored in the game tree without affecting the outcome, making it particularly useful for complex games like Chess. Another key method involves the use of heuristic functions, which estimate the quality of a game state without fully exploring the game tree. These heuristics guide decision-making by prioritizing promising moves, significantly speeding up the process, especially in games with large state spaces. For instance, in Chess, heuristics might evaluate material advantage, piece positioning, and board control to determine the best move without exhaustively analyzing all possibilities.

Reinforcement learning has revolutionized AI in game playing by enabling agents to learn optimal strategies through repeated gameplay. By interacting with the environment and receiving rewards or penalties for their actions, agents refine their strategies over time. This approach has been pivotal in training AI to excel in games like Go, Poker, and Dota 2, where traditional rule-based approaches struggle due to the complexity and variability of these games. For stochastic games, Monte Carlo methods provide a probabilistic framework to estimate the likelihood of success for a move. By simulating numerous random game plays from a given state, these methods identify moves with the highest expected value. Advanced AI systems like AlphaGo have taken game playing to new heights by combining deep learning with traditional techniques. Using neural networks, these systems evaluate game states and learn strategies directly from vast amounts of gameplay data, enabling them to outperform human champions in games of immense complexity and subtlety.

These techniques collectively enable AI systems to make intelligent, adaptive decisions in games, serving as a foundation for broader applications in real-world problem-solving domains.

Applications of Game Playing AI

AI has made significant contributions to recreational gaming, where it powers non-player characters (NPCs) and opponents in video games and board games. By leveraging advanced algorithms, AI creates challenging and adaptive gameplay experiences for human players. For example, in strategy games, AI opponents can analyze the player's moves and adjust their strategies dynamically, providing a competitive and engaging environment. These applications enhance entertainment value and offer players opportunities to improve their skills by facing increasingly sophisticated virtual adversaries. In the domain of education and training, AI-driven games are used as effective tools to teach critical skills such as strategic thinking, problem-solving, and decision-making. Educational games simulate real-world scenarios, enabling learners to experiment with strategies and assess their outcomes in a risk-free environment. In military training, AI-based simulations prepare personnel for complex decision-making under pressure, such as managing battlefield logistics or coordinating missions. These applications demonstrate how game-playing AI can transcend entertainment to deliver practical, skill-building benefits.

AI techniques developed for games have also found applications in strategic planning across industries. For instance, the same algorithms used to plan moves in Chess or Go are employed in business strategy, financial modeling, and supply chain optimization. These techniques help organizations predict outcomes, optimize resource allocation, and develop long-term strategies. By modeling these real-world challenges as decision-making problems similar to games, AI provides innovative solutions that enhance efficiency and competitiveness. In cognitive science, studying AI in games offers insights into human intelligence and decision-making processes. Researchers use AI models to simulate human behavior in game-playing scenarios, shedding light on how people approach complex problems, evaluate risks, and develop strategies. These findings inform the design of AI systems that can collaborate with humans, mimic human-like reasoning, or even improve upon it, making game-playing AI an invaluable tool for advancing our understanding of cognition and artificial intelligence.

Challenges in Game Playing AI

While game-playing AI has achieved remarkable success, it still faces challenges. Real-world games often have enormous state spaces, making exhaustive search infeasible. Games involving imperfect information or stochastic elements require sophisticated probabilistic reasoning. Additionally, designing AI that can adapt to human players' unpredictable strategies remains an ongoing research area. Game playing continues to be a dynamic and impactful field in AI, bridging the gap between theoretical research and practical applications. From the early days of Chess-playing programs to modern systems like AlphaGo and OpenAI's Dota 2 bots, advancements in game-playing AI reflect broader progress in artificial intelligence as a whole.

Min-max and alpha-beta Pruning Algorithms

Min-Max Algorithm

The Min-Max algorithm is a decision-making strategy used in artificial intelligence for game playing. It is designed for two-player, zero-sum games where one player's gain is the other player's loss. The goal of the algorithm is to find the best possible move for the maximizing player (usually the AI) while assuming that the opponent (minimizing player) will also play optimally.The algorithm works by exploring the game tree, evaluating all possible moves, and assigning a value to each node based on the potential outcomes. At each level of the tree, the algorithm alternates between the maximizing player, who tries to maximize the score, and the minimizing player, who tries to minimize it. The Min-Max algorithm guarantees the best outcome for the maximizing player if both players play optimally. However, its computational complexity grows exponentially with the depth of the game tree, making it inefficient for large games.

Alpha-Beta Pruning Algorithm

Alpha-Beta pruning is an optimization of the Min-Max algorithm. It reduces the number of nodes evaluated in the game tree, making the search process more efficient without affecting the outcome. The algorithm introduces two parameters:

- Alpha: The best score that the maximizing player can guarantee at that point.
- Beta: The best score that the minimizing player can guarantee at that point.

The pruning process involves ignoring branches of the tree that cannot affect the final decision. If a node's value is worse than a previously explored path for the maximizing or minimizing player, that branch is skipped. This dramatically reduces the computational complexity, allowing the algorithm to explore deeper levels of the game tree within the same time constraints. Comparison on Min-Max vs. Alpha-Beta Pruningmention in below Table 2.4:

Table 2.4: Min-Max vs. Alpha-Beta Pruning

Feature	Min-Max Algorithm	Alpha-Beta Pruning
Purpose	Finds the optimal move in a two-player game	Optimizes the Min-Max algorithm
Efficiency	Explores the entire game tree	Prunes unnecessary branches
Parameters	None	Uses alpha and beta values
Space Complexity	O(b^d)	O(b^d), same as Min-Max
Time Complexity	O(b^d), where b = branching factor, d = depth	O(b^(d/2)) with effective pruning

Example of Alpha-Beta Pruning

Consider a game tree where the maximizing player (AI) and minimizing player alternate turns:

Start Evaluation:

The maximizing player starts at the root node, and the algorithm begins exploring the game tree.

Alpha and Beta Updates:

As the algorithm evaluates each node, it updates the alpha and beta values to reflect the best scores seen so far for each player.

Pruning:

If a node's value is outside the range defined by alpha and beta, the algorithm skips further evaluation of that branch, saving computational effort.

Result:

The algorithm selects the optimal move for the maximizing player, considering only the most promising branches.

The Min-Max algorithm provides a foundational approach for game-playing AI, while Alpha-Beta pruning enhances its efficiency, enabling practical application to complex games.

Conclusion

Problem-solving and searching techniques in artificial intelligence (AI) involve systematic methods to explore and resolve complex tasks. These techniques begin with understanding problem characteristics and modeling problems using production systems and appropriate control strategies. Core methods include Breadth-First Search and Depth-First Search, foundational approaches for exhaustive exploration. Advanced techniques like Hill Climbing and its variations enhance efficiency by focusing on local optimizations, while Heuristic Search Techniques like Best-First Search and the A Algorithm* incorporate domain knowledge for faster decision-making. Constraint Satisfaction Problems (CSPs) formalize problems with variables and constraints, while Means-End Analysis iteratively reduces the difference between the current and goal states. In game playing, strategies such as Min-Max and Alpha-Beta Pruning are employed to optimize decisions in competitive environments. These techniques underpin AI's ability to solve real-world challenges, from pathfinding to strategic planning and intelligent decision-making. Next Chapter explores into the fundamental concepts of Knowledge Representation, exploring techniques such as Propositional Logic and First-Order Predicate Logic for expressing knowledge. It covers advanced topics like the Resolution Principle, Unification, and structured representation methods including Semantic Nets, Conceptual Dependencies, Frames, and Scripts, alongside production rules. The chapter concludes with an introduction to Programming in Logic (PROLOG), providing a practical perspective on implementing knowledge-based systems.

Exercise:

- Define the characteristics of a well-structured problem and explain how these influence problem-solving strategies.
- Describe the role of a production system in AI and provide an example of its application.
- Compare and contrast Breadth-First Search and Depth-First Search in terms of space and time complexity.
- Explain how Hill Climbing works and discuss its limitations in finding optimal solutions.
- What is a heuristic function, and how does it improve the efficiency of search techniques like A Algorithm*?
- Solve a simple CSP for a Sudoku problem with a 3x3 grid, providing a step-by-step explanation.
- Describe the process of Means-End Analysis with an example from robotics or navigation.
- Discuss the differences between Best-First Search and A Algorithm*, and explain their advantages in pathfinding problems.
- Illustrate how Alpha-Beta Pruning optimizes the Min-Max Algorithm with an example game tree.

Write a program or pseudocode to implement the Min-Max Algorithm with Alpha-Beta pruning for a Tic-Tac-Toe game.

3

Knowledge Representation

Introduction

This chapter introduces the principles of Knowledge Representation, a crucial area in AI for encoding information about the world in a form that machines can process. It covers logical approaches like Propositional Logic and First-Order Predicate Logic, structured representations such as Semantic Nets, Frames, and Scripts, and practical tools like PROLOG for implementing intelligent systems.

Objective

The objective of this chapter is to provide an understanding of different knowledge representation techniques and their applications in AI. It aims to equip readers with the skills to model knowledge logically, resolve logical inferences, and apply structured and programming-based approaches to develop intelligent systems.

Propositional Logic

Propositional Logic, also known as propositional calculus or sentential logic, is a branch of logic that focuses on the relationships between propositions—statements that are either true or false but never both. It provides a formal framework for reasoning, where propositions are combined using logical connectives such as AND (∧), OR (∨), NOT (¬), IMPLIES (→), and EQUIVALENT (↔). These connectives allow the creation of more complex expressions, enabling systems to represent relationships and dependencies between individual facts. Propositional logic serves as the foundation for reasoning in artificial intelligence (AI), making it possible to model and infer conclusions about simple knowledge domains. At the heart of propositional logic lies its formal structure, defined by syntax and semantics. Syntax specifies the rules for constructing valid logical statements, while semantics assigns truth values to propositions and defines how the truth of complex expressions depends on their components. For example, the truth of a compound statement $P \wedge Q$ (P AND Q) depends on both P and Q being true. Propositional logic uses truth tables to evaluate logical expressions systematically, making it a powerful tool for automated reasoning and problem-solving in AI. Despite its strengths, propositional logic has limitations in its expressiveness. It is well-suited for representing basic facts and rules but cannot handle more complex scenarios involving objects, relationships, or quantifiers (e.g., "All humans are mortal"). For such cases, more advanced systems like First-Order Predicate Logic are required. Nevertheless, propositional logic remains a critical building block in AI, widely used in knowledge representation, decision-making, and automated reasoning.

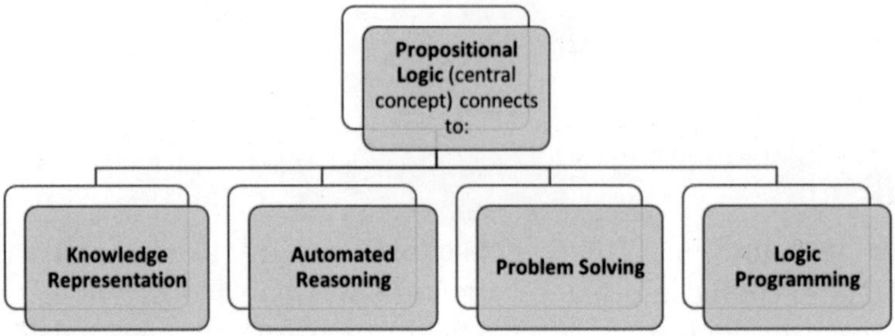

Block diagram illustrating the applications of Propositional Logic in AI, highlighting its key uses in Knowledge Representation, Automated Reasoning, Problem Solving, and Logic Programming.

Components of Propositional Logic

Propositions:

Propositions are atomic units in propositional logic that can either be true (T) or false (F).

Examples:

"It is raining." (True or False)

"2 + 2 = 4." (Always True)

Logical Connectives:

AND (∧): Combines two propositions and is true only if both are true.

$P \wedge Q$**:** True if

$P=T$ and $Q=T$.

OR (∨): Combines two propositions and is true if at least one is true.

$P \vee Q$: True if $P=T$, $Q=T$, or both.

NOT (¬): Negates the truth value of a proposition.

$\neg P$**:** True if

$P=F$, False if

$P=T$.

IMPLIES (→): Represents implication, where

$P \rightarrow Q$is false only if

$P=T$ and $Q=F$.

EQUIVALENT (↔): Represents equivalence, where

$P \leftrightarrow Q$ is true if P and Q

Q have the same truth value.

Syntax and Semantics:

Syntax defines the rules for forming valid statements.

Example:

$(P \wedge Q) \rightarrow R \rightarrow$R is a valid formula.

Semantics assigns truth values to propositions and defines how complex formulas evaluate based on their components.

Truth Tables

Truth tables systematically represent the truth values of logical expressions for all possible combinations of their components. For example:

AND (∧):

PPP	QQQ	P∧QP ∧ QP∧Q
True	True	True
True	False	False
False	True	False
False	False	False

IMPLIES (→):

PPP	QQQ	P→QP → QP→Q
True	True	True
True	False	False
False	True	True
False	False	True

Applications of Propositional Logic in AI

Propositional logic is extensively used in artificial intelligence for various applications. One key area is knowledge representation, where it encodes simple facts and rules about the world. For instance, let P: "It is raining" and Q: "The ground is wet." Using propositional logic, the relationship between these facts can be expressed as $P \rightarrow Q$, meaning "If it is raining, then the ground is wet." This logical framework enables AI systems to represent and manipulate knowledge systematically. Another significant application is in automated reasoning, where logical systems use inference rules like Modus Ponens to deduce new information. For example, given $P \rightarrow Q$ (If P, then Q) and P (It is raining), the system can infer Q (The ground is wet). Propositional logic provides a foundation for such reasoning, enabling AI to draw conclusions based on existing knowledge. Additionally, it plays a vital role in problem solving tasks, such as planning and diagnosis, by encoding problems and reasoning through logical steps to identify solutions. Furthermore, propositional logic forms the basis of logic programming languages like PROLOG, which are widely used for building intelligent systems.

Advantages of Propositional Logic

Propositional logic offers several advantages that make it a valuable tool in AI. Its simplicity ensures that it is easy to understand and use, with well-defined syntax and semantics. It provides a robust framework for formal reasoning, allowing AI systems to reason about truth and derive conclusions systematically. Additionally, it is highly expressive for simple scenarios, making it effective for representing basic facts and relationships in structured environments.

Limitations of Propositional Logic

Despite its usefulness, propositional logic has notable limitations. One major drawback is its lack of expressiveness; it cannot represent complex relationships involving objects, properties, or quantifiers, such as "All cats are mammals." For such scenarios, more advanced logical systems like First-Order Predicate Logic are required. Another challenge is scalability; as the number of propositions and rules grows, reasoning and computation can become increasingly expensive, limiting its applicability to large and complex systems. Propositional logic remains a fundamental component of AI, providing a strong foundation for reasoning and problem-solving, but its limitations often necessitate the use of more advanced systems for complex applications.

First-Order Predicate Logic

First-Order Predicate Logic (FOPL), also known as First-Order Logic (FOL), is an advanced formal system that builds upon propositional logic by introducing variables, quantifiers, predicates, and functions. Unlike propositional logic, which deals with simple declarative statements, FOPL enables reasoning about objects, their properties, and relationships. This expressive capability makes FOPL a critical tool in AI for representing complex knowledge and performing logical reasoning.

Components of First-Order Predicate Logic

The fundamental elements of FOPL include constants, variables, predicates, functions, quantifiers, and logical connectives. Constants represent specific objects in the domain, such as "John" or "Earth." Variables act as placeholders that can represent any object within the domain, such as x or y. Predicates describe properties or relationships among objects, for example,

$Likes(John, Pizza)$, which means "John likes pizza." Functions map objects to other objects, such as $Father(John)$, which could represent "John's father."

FOPL also introduces quantifiers to specify the scope of a statement. The Universal Quantifier (∀) expresses that a statement applies to all objects in the domain, such as ∀ x Loves(x,Mother), meaning "Everyone loves their mother." The Existential Quantifier (∃) asserts that a statement applies to at least one object, such as $\exists x Likes(x,Pizza)$, meaning "Someone likes pizza." Logical connectives such as AND (∧), OR (∨), and NOT (¬) are used to combine and manipulate statements, similar to propositional logic.

Syntax and Semantics

The syntax of FOPL defines the rules for constructing valid logical formulas. An atomic formula in FOPL consists of a predicate applied to terms, such as $Human(Socrates)$. Complex formulas are built using logical connectives and quantifiers, as in $\forall x(Human(x) \rightarrow Mortal(x))$, meaning "All humans are mortal." Semantics, on the other hand, assign truth values to these formulas based on their interpretation in a given domain. For example, if the domain includes "Socrates" as a human, and "Mortal" applies to all humans, then $Mortal(Socrates)$Socrates) evaluates to true.

Advantages of FOPL

FOPL offers a significant advantage in its expressiveness, allowing it to represent complex relationships and generalizations that propositional logic cannot handle. For instance, it can represent statements like "All humans are mortal," which involves universal quantification over a set of objects. Its ability to reason about relationships among objects enables it to model hierarchical knowledge effectively, such as "A teacher is also a person." Additionally, the support for quantifiers makes FOPL ideal for capturing both generalizations and specific instances, enhancing its versatility in knowledge representation.

Limitations of FOPL

Despite its strengths, FOPL has certain limitations. One major drawback is its computational complexity, as reasoning with FOPL can be computationally expensive and, in some cases, undecidable. Another limitation is its reliance on a fixed domain of discourse, which must be predefined and cannot dynamically accommodate new objects or relationships. Finally, FOPL assumes precise and complete knowledge, which is often unrealistic in real-world applications where uncertainty and incomplete information are common.

Example of FOPL in AI

Consider the classic logical reasoning example: "All humans are mortal. Socrates is a human. Therefore, Socrates is mortal." This can be represented in FOPL as follows:

- $\forall x(\text{Human}(x) \rightarrow \text{Mortal}(x))$: "All humans are mortal."
- Human(Socrates): "Socrates is a human."
- Using the inference rule Modus Ponens, we can deduce
- Mortal(Socrates): "Socrates is mortal."

This example demonstrates how FOPL combines universal quantification and logical inference to derive meaningful conclusions from a set of premises.

Applications of FOPL in AI

FOPL is widely applied across various AI domains. In knowledge-based systems, it represents and reasons about facts and relationships in expert systems, such as medical diagnosis. In natural language processing (NLP), FOPL provides a semantic framework for interpreting sentences and reasoning about their meanings. In automated theorem proving, FOPL is used to prove mathematical theorems by applying logical inference rules. Additionally, in robotics, FOPL represents and reasons about the environment and tasks, enabling robots to plan and execute actions effectively.

Table: Features of First-Order Predicate Logic (FOPL)

Feature	Description in FOPL
Representation	Uses predicates, functions, constants, and variables to represent objects and relationships.
Quantifiers	Supports universal (∀) and existential (∃) quantifiers for generalizations and specific cases.
Complexity	Computationally complex and can be undecidable in certain cases.
Expressiveness	Highly expressive, able to represent complex relationships and hierarchical knowledge.
Applications	Used in knowledge-based systems, natural language processing, automated reasoning, and robotics.

First-Order Predicate Logic is a powerful and expressive tool for representing and reasoning about complex knowledge in AI. Its ability to handle variables, quantifiers, and relationships makes it far more versatile than propositional logic. While it has limitations, such as computational complexity and fixed domain assumptions, FOPL remains a foundational framework in AI for tasks requiring formal reasoning and structured knowledge representation.

Resolution Principle

The Resolution Principle is a powerful inference technique in logic that provides a systematic way to derive conclusions or prove the validity of statements. It is extensively used in Propositional Logic and First-Order Predicate Logic (FOPL) for automated reasoning, particularly in theorem proving and knowledge representation. The core idea of the resolution principle is to iteratively combine pairs of logical statements containing complementary literals to derive new conclusions or detect inconsistencies. If a contradiction, represented as an empty clause, is derived, the negation of the goal is refuted, and the original statement is proven true. Resolution is both sound (it only derives conclusions that are logically valid) and complete (it can derive all conclusions that are logically entailed). These properties make it a cornerstone of logic-based AI systems. By systematically reducing complex logical expressions into simpler components, the resolution principle enables AI to reason about facts, rules, and relationships effectively.

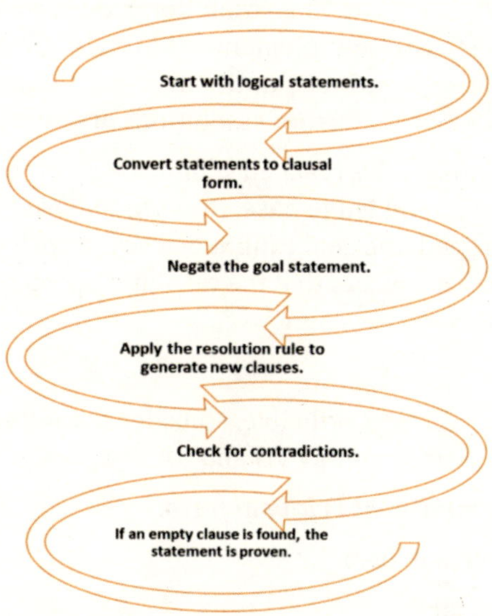

block diagram representing the Resolution Principle

Concepts of the Resolution Principle

A fundamental requirement for applying the resolution principle is the conversion of logical statements into clausal form. Clausal form is a standardized representation where statements are expressed as a conjunction of disjunctions of literals. For example, the statement $P \rightarrow Q$ ("If

P, then Q") can be converted into $\neg P \vee Q$. Literals are atomic propositions or their negations, and a clause is a disjunction of literals.

The process of unification plays a critical role in resolving clauses in First-Order Logic. Unification involves substituting variables with constants or other variables to make two literals complementary, enabling their resolution. For instance, Likes(x,y) and Likes(John,y) can be unified by substituting x=John. Complementary literals, such as P and $\neg P$, are eliminated during resolution to form a new clause, simplifying the logical expression.

Steps in Applying the Resolution Principle

The resolution principle operates through a structured series of steps. First, all logical statements are converted into clausal form by eliminating implications, moving negations inward using De Morgan's laws, and rewriting the statements as disjunctions of literals. For example, a statement like $\forall x(P(x) \rightarrow Q(x))$ is transformed into $\neg P(x) \vee Q(x)$.

The next step is to negate the goal statement that needs to be proven and add it to the set of known clauses. For instance, if the goal is Q, its negation $\neg Q$ is added to the knowledge base. The resolution rule is then applied iteratively, where pairs of clauses with complementary literals are resolved to produce new clauses. This process continues until either an empty clause (indicating a contradiction) is derived or no further resolutions are possible.

When an empty clause (□) is reached, it indicates that the negation of the goal is inconsistent with the knowledge base, proving the original goal statement. If no contradiction is derived, the goal cannot be proven with the given knowledge. This systematic approach ensures that the resolution principle can handle a wide range of logical problems.

Example

To illustrate the resolution principle, consider the following example: Prove that Q is true, given the statements $P \vee Q$ and $\neg P$.

Convert the statements into clausal form:

$P \vee Q$: Already in clausal form.

$\neg P$: Already in clausal form.

Negate the goal Q: Add $\neg Q$ to the knowledge base.

Apply resolution:

Resolve $P \vee Q$ with $\neg Q$ to eliminate Q, producing P.

Resolve

P with $\neg P$ to eliminate P, producing the empty clause (□).

Applications of the Resolution Principle

The resolution principle is widely used in various fields of artificial intelligence and computer science. One of its primary applications is in automated theorem proving, where it serves as the basis for algorithms that validate logical proofs.

Systems like Prolog use resolution to deduce conclusions from a set of logical rules and facts.In knowledge representation and reasoning, resolution enables AI systems to infer new knowledge from existing data. For instance, in an expert system, resolution can derive conclusions about medical diagnoses or equipment faults based on a set of rules and observed symptoms. It is also instrumental in natural language processing (NLP), where it helps validate semantic relationships and ensure logical consistency in sentence interpretation.Additionally, the resolution principle is employed in problem-solving applications such as planning and diagnostics, where AI systems need to reason through complex scenarios to identify causes and solutions. Its systematic and logical approach makes it an invaluable tool for tasks requiring precision and rigor.

Advantages of the Resolution Principle

The resolution principle offers several advantages that make it a cornerstone of logic-based AI systems. Its soundness ensures that any conclusion derived using the principle is logically valid, while its completeness guarantees that all logically entailed conclusions can be derived. This dual property makes resolution a reliable method for reasoning and inference.Another advantage is its systematic approach, which provides a clear framework for deducing conclusions. The resolution principle reduces complex logical problems into smaller, manageable steps, making it suitable for automation in AI systems. Furthermore, its application across different domains, from theorem proving to diagnostics, highlights its versatility.

Limitations of the Resolution Principle

Despite its strengths, the resolution principle has certain limitations. One significant drawback is its computational complexity, as the number of clauses and potential resolutions can grow exponentially with the size of the knowledge base. This makes it resource-intensive for large and complex problems. Furthermore, the principle relies on the conversion of logical statements into clausal form, which can increase the size and complexity of the problem. This dependency can lead to inefficiencies, particularly in cases where the clausal form becomes unwieldy. Another limitation is its assumption of deterministic and complete knowledge, which restricts its applicability in real-world scenarios involving uncertainty or incomplete information.

Unification

Unification is a fundamental concept in first-order predicate logic and automated reasoning. It is a process of making two logical expressions identical by finding a substitution of variables that makes their structure and content equivalent. This mechanism is essential in systems that rely on reasoning, such as Prolog and theorem provers, as it enables matching of logical expressions and facilitates inference. Unification works by comparing two expressions, called terms, which can be constants, variables, functions, or combinations thereof. If a substitution exists that makes the two terms identical, they are said to unify. For example, given the terms Loves(x,Mary) and Loves(John,y), the unifier x=John,y=Mary makes the terms identical as Loves(John,Mary). Unification is often used as a step in applying inference rules like Modus Ponens and resolution in predicate logic.

Components of Unification

The process of unification revolves around the unifier, which is the set of substitutions needed to make two terms identical. A substitution replaces variables in a term with other terms, such as constants or variables. For instance, {x/John} is a substitution that replaces x with $John$. A unifier is considered most general if it contains the minimum necessary substitutions, leaving as many variables as possible to retain their generality.

For example, for P(x) and P(y), the most general unifier (MGU) is {x/y}.

Unification operates recursively, breaking down expressions into smaller components until all corresponding parts are matched. Constants must match exactly, variables can be substituted with any term, and functions must have the same name and arity (number of arguments) to unify.

How Unification Works?

The unification algorithm systematically compares the components of two terms. If the terms are identical, they are already unified. If one term is a variable and the other is any term, the variable is substituted with the term.

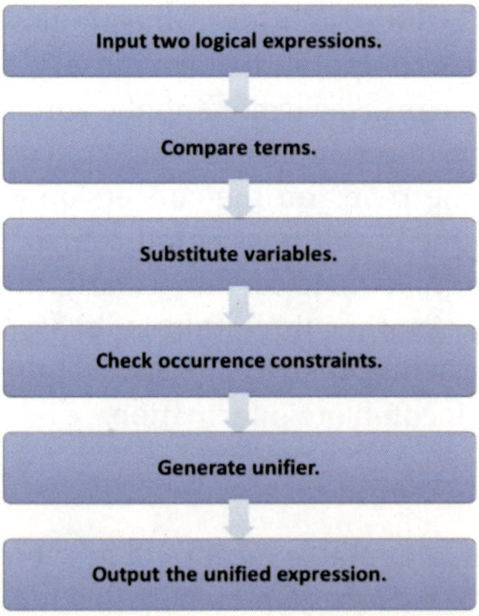

lock diagram representing the workflow of Unification in logic

For example, x and Loves(John,Mary) unify with {x/Loves(John,Mary)}. When both terms are functions, their names and arguments are compared recursively. If there is a conflict (e.g.,Loves(x,Mary) and Hates(x,Mary)), unification fails.

Unification also checks for occurrence constraints, ensuring that a variable is not substituted with a term containing itself. For example, x and Loves(x,Mary) cannot unify, as x would appear infinitely in the substitution. This constraint prevents circular substitutions and ensures the validity of unification.

Applications of Unification

Unification plays a crucial role in various fields of artificial intelligence. In logic programming languages like Prolog, unification is used to match goals with rules in the knowledge base. For instance, a query Loves(John,Mary) can be matched with a rule Loves(x,y) using the unifier {x/John,y/Mary}. This enables the system to infer new facts or prove the validity of a query.

In theorem proving, unification is used in the resolution principle to identify complementary literals and resolve them. For example, resolving Loves (x,Mary) and¬Loves (John,y) requires the unifier {x/John,y/Mary}. Additionally, unification is applied in natural language processing (NLP) for tasks like semantic interpretation, where matching linguistic structures is necessary for understanding and reasoning.

Advantages and Limitations

Unification offers a systematic and efficient method for reasoning in logical systems. Its ability to generalize and find commonality between terms makes it a cornerstone of inference mechanisms in AI. However, it has limitations. For example, unification assumes deterministic and complete knowledge, which may not always hold in real-world scenarios. Moreover, the process can become computationally expensive for complex terms or large knowledge bases.Despite its challenges, unification remains an essential tool in artificial intelligence, enabling systems to reason about knowledge, match patterns, and make inferences. Its role in logic programming, automated reasoning, and natural language understanding underscores its importance in building intelligent systems.

Semantic Nets

Semantic Nets (or Semantic Networks) are a graphical knowledge representation technique used in artificial intelligence (AI) to model relationships between objects, concepts, and ideas. They represent information as a network of nodes and edges, where nodes correspond to entities or concepts, and edges denote relationships between them. Semantic nets offer an intuitive and flexible way to encode structured knowledge, allowing AI systems to traverse the network for reasoning and inference. This method is widely used in applications like natural language processing (NLP), cognitive modeling, and expert systems.

A fundamental feature of semantic nets is the use of labeled edges to define specific types of relationships, such as "is-a" (hierarchical classification) or "has-part" (composition). For example, a semantic net might represent that a "Dog" is a "Mammal" and that it "has-part" a "Tail." By organizing knowledge into a graph-like structure, semantic nets facilitate understanding and manipulation of complex relationships, making them a versatile tool in AI.

Structure of Semantic Nets

Semantic nets are structured as directed graphs with nodes and edges:

- Nodes: Represent entities, concepts, or objects.
- Example: "Dog," "Animal," or "Tail."
- Edges: Represent relationships between nodes.
- Example: "is-a" for hierarchical relationships, or "has-part" for compositional ones.

Attributes can also be attached to nodes or edges to encode additional information, such as weights, probabilities, or conditions. For instance, a semantic net might represent "Dog" →can-do "Bark," where "can-do" defines a functional relationship. Moreover, transitive relationships enable reasoning across multiple edges, such as deducing that a "Dog" is an "Animal" if a "Dog" is a "Mammal" and a "Mammal" is an "Animal."

Advantages and Applications

Semantic nets have several advantages. They are highly intuitive and easy to visualize, making them accessible for both humans and machines. Their graph-based structure allows for efficient traversal algorithms to infer new relationships or verify existing ones.

For example,

If:

$$A \xrightarrow{\text{is-a}} B$$

and:

$$B \xrightarrow{\text{is-a}} C$$

then the system can infer:

$$A \xrightarrow{\text{is-a}} C$$

This makes semantic nets ideal for reasoning tasks.

Applications of semantic nets span various AI fields:

- Natural Language Processing (NLP): Used to represent meanings of words and their relationships for tasks like text understanding and machine translation.

- Expert Systems: Serve as the backbone of knowledge bases in fields such as medical diagnosis or technical troubleshooting.
- Ontology Modeling: Semantic nets are instrumental in creating ontologies to formalize relationships within specific domains.
- Cognitive Science: Model human memory and associative thought processes by representing how concepts are linked in the brain.

Challenges and Limitations

Despite their benefits, semantic nets face challenges. As the size and complexity of the network grow, managing and computing relationships becomes increasingly difficult. For example, large semantic nets may suffer from scalability issues, requiring advanced algorithms to maintain efficiency. Additionally, semantic nets do not inherently handle ambiguity or uncertainty, which are common in real-world knowledge. Extensions such as weighted semantic nets or probabilistic approaches are needed to address these limitations. Another limitation lies in the dynamic nature of knowledge. Updating semantic nets in response to new information can be complex and may require restructuring the network. Despite these challenges, semantic nets remain a foundational approach in AI, particularly when combined with complementary techniques to enhance their functionality.

Example Table: Semantic Net Representation

Node	Relationship	Target Node	Meaning
Dog	is-a	Mammal	A dog is a mammal.
Mammal	is-a	Animal	A mammal is an animal.
Dog	has-part	Tail	A dog has a tail.
Dog	can-do	Bark	A dog can bark.
Animal	needs	Food	Animals need food.

This table illustrates a simple semantic net with nodes (e.g., "Dog," "Mammal") and edges (e.g., "is-a," "has-part") that define relationships between concepts.

Conceptual Dependencies

Conceptual Dependencies (CD) is a knowledge representation technique developed by Roger Schank in the 1970s to represent the meaning of natural language sentences. The primary goal of CDs is to create a language-independent framework for understanding and reasoning about events, actions, and their relationships. This representation uses a structured format to depict the underlying semantics of a sentence rather than its syntactic form, making it useful for natural language understanding and inference in AI.CDs are designed to capture the essential meaning of a statement, focusing on actions (verbs), participants (nouns), and their roles. The approach relies on a set of primitive actions and predefined relationships, ensuring that sentences with the same meaning but different syntactic structures are represented in a consistent way. For example, "John gave Mary a book" and "Mary received a book from John" would have the same conceptual dependency representation.

Components of Conceptual Dependencies

- Primitive Actions: CDs define a set of primitive actions that form the building blocks of all events. These primitives include actions like transfer of possession (ATRANS), physical movement (PTRANS), transfer of information (MTRANS), and transfer of energy (INGEST). Each action represents a fundamental type of activity or change.
- Conceptual Roles: Each action is associated with specific roles, such as the actor, object, recipient, and instrument. For example, in the action "John gave a book to Mary," "John" is the actor, "book" is the object, and "Mary" is the recipient.
- Dependencies: CDs connect these components to represent the relationships between actions and their participants. Dependencies can represent causality, purpose, or temporal relationships, enabling the system to reason about the sequence and logic of events.
- Focus on Meaning: By abstracting away from surface-level syntax, CDs allow AI systems to focus on the core semantics of a sentence. This enables better reasoning, as the representation captures the essential meaning rather than the specific words used.

Representation Format

Conceptual dependencies are represented using a graphical or tabular format. Each event or action is represented as a structure with labeled links connecting the components. For example:

Sentence: "John gave Mary a book."

CD Representation:

Action:

ATRANS (transfer of possession)

Actor: John

Object: Book

Recipient: Mary

In a graph, this might look like:

ATRANS as the central node.

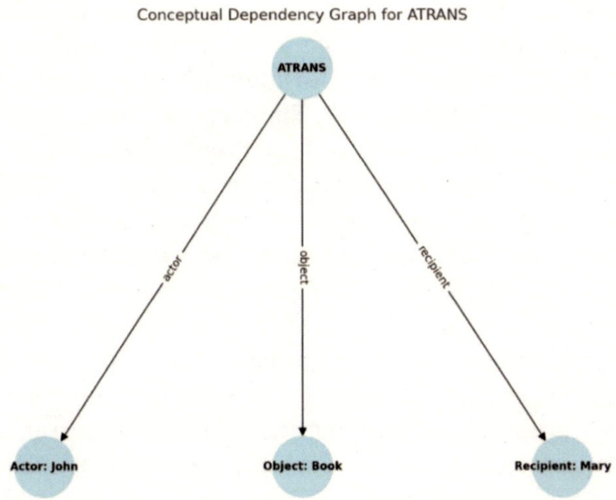

Arrows labeled "actor," "object," and "recipient" pointing to their respective entities.

The structured format ensures that even complex sentences can be broken down into manageable, machine-readable components for reasoning.

Advantages of Conceptual Dependencies

Language Independence and Inference Facilitation: Conceptual Dependencies (CDs) provide a universal framework for representing knowledge by abstracting away from specific languages. This language-independent approach allows systems to process input from multiple languages seamlessly and even translate between them. By explicitly modeling the relationships between actions and participants, CDs facilitate inference, enabling AI systems to deduce additional details or fill in gaps. For instance, given "John gave Mary a book," the system can infer that "John no longer has the book," showcasing the ability to reason about implicit information. Consistency and Expressiveness: CDs offer a uniform representation of sentences with similar meanings, irrespective of their syntactic structure. This standardization simplifies reasoning and knowledge retrieval, as sentences like "John gave Mary a book" and "Mary received a book from John" are represented identically. Furthermore, CDs are richly expressive, capturing intricate details like causality, purpose, and temporal relationships. This enables AI systems to perform sophisticated reasoning about events, their contexts, and interdependencies, making CDs a powerful tool for understanding and reasoning in AI.

Applications of Conceptual Dependencies

Natural Language Understanding and Story Comprehension: Conceptual Dependencies (CDs) play a crucial role in systems designed to process and reason about natural language, such as virtual assistants and conversational AI. By representing the underlying semantics of language rather than its surface structure, CDs enable these systems to interpret user inputs more effectively and generate meaningful responses. Similarly, in story understanding, CDs break down narratives into events and relationships, making it easier for AI to comprehend complex sequences and infer unstated details. This capability has been successfully applied in tasks like automated storytelling, where AI creates coherent narratives, and text summarization, where AI condenses content while preserving its meaning. Knowledge-Based Systems and Robotics: In expert systems, CDs provide a structured way to represent rules and facts about real-world processes, enabling robust reasoning and decision-making. For example, a medical diagnosis system can use CDs to model symptoms and their causal relationships to diseases. In AI planning and robotics, CDs are employed to model and execute sequences of actions in dynamic environments. They help systems reason about causality and purpose, ensuring that robots can adapt their behavior to achieve goals efficiently. This makes CDs indispensable in domains where understanding and executing complex processes are critical.

Frames, and Scripts

Frames and Scripts are structured knowledge representation techniques used in artificial intelligence (AI) to organize and reason about information in an intuitive manner. These techniques help AI systems manage both static and dynamic knowledge, making them essential for understanding and interacting with the world.

Frames

Frames were introduced by Marvin Minsky as a way to represent static knowledge about concepts, objects, or situations. A frame is essentially a data structure consisting of slots and fillers. Slots represent attributes or properties, while fillers provide specific values for these attributes. For instance, a "Car" frame might have slots like "Make," "Model," "Color," and "Owner," with fillers providing details such as "Toyota," "Corolla," "Red," and "John," respectively. Frames also support inheritance, where child frames inherit properties from parent frames. For example, a "Sports Car" frame can inherit attributes from the "Car" frame while adding unique properties like "Top Speed." This hierarchical structure simplifies reasoning and reduces redundancy. Frames are particularly effective in domains like object recognition, expert systems, and natural language understanding, where structured and hierarchical representation is required.

Scripts

Scripts, introduced by Roger Schank, represent dynamic knowledge about sequences of events or actions that typically occur in specific situations. Unlike frames, which focus on static attributes, scripts focus on temporal and causal relationships between actions. For example, a "Restaurant Script" might describe the sequence of actions involved in dining at a restaurant, including "Entering," "Ordering Food," "Eating," and "Paying the Bill." Scripts consist of components like entry conditions (preconditions for the script to start), roles (participants in the events), scenes (sub-events or actions), props (objects involved), and results (expected outcomes). By encapsulating common event sequences, scripts enable AI systems to predict and understand behaviors in dynamic contexts, such as understanding customer interactions in a service setting.

Comparison of Frames and Scripts

While both frames and scripts are powerful knowledge representation tools, they serve different purposes. Frames are ideal for representing static knowledge about objects and concepts, while scripts are suited for modeling dynamic, event-driven scenarios. For instance, a frame can represent the static properties of a "Restaurant," while a script captures the sequence of events that occur when dining at the restaurant.

Example Table: Frames vs. Scripts

Feature	Frames	Scripts
Purpose	Represent static knowledge.	Represent dynamic, event-driven knowledge.
Structure	Attributes (slots) with values (fillers).	Sequences of events or actions.
Inheritance	Supported, hierarchical.	Not applicable.
Applications	Objects, concepts, and hierarchies.	Event-based scenarios and processes.
Example	"Car: Make: Toyota, Model: Corolla."	"Customer orders food at a restaurant."

Production Rules

Production Rules are a widely used knowledge representation technique in artificial intelligence (AI) for encoding decision-making processes. They consist of a set of conditional statements, often written in an IF (Condition) THEN (Action) format, which define how a system transitions from one state to another or performs specific actions based on input data. This method is particularly effective in rule-based and expert systems, providing a structured and interpretable way to represent domain knowledge. The condition (also called the antecedent) specifies the criteria that must be satisfied for the rule to apply, while the action (or consequent) defines the response if the condition holds true. For example, in a temperature control system, a rule might state, "IF the temperature is below 20°C, THEN turn on the heater." Rules can also include multiple conditions combined using logical operators like AND, OR, and NOT, enabling the representation of complex logic.

How Production Rules Work?

Production rules operate through a cycle of matching, conflict resolution, and execution. In the matching phase, the system evaluates the conditions of all rules against the current state or data. If multiple rules are applicable, a conflict resolution mechanism selects one rule based on predefined criteria, such as priority or recency. Once a rule is selected, the corresponding action is executed, which might modify the system's state or produce an output. This cycle repeats until no more rules are applicable or a predefined goal is achieved. This operational approach allows systems to dynamically adapt to changes in input and state.

There are two primary reasoning methods for applying production rules: forward chaining and backward chaining. Forward chaining starts with known facts and applies rules iteratively to infer new facts or conclusions. For example, in a medical diagnosis system, symptoms (facts) are matched against rules to infer possible diseases. Backward chaining, on the other hand, begins with a goal and works backward to determine if the conditions for the goal are satisfied. For instance, to determine loan eligibility, the system starts with the goal "Loan Approved" and checks if conditions like income or credit history are met.

Production rules work:

1. Start: Begin the cycle.

2. Match Conditions: Evaluate the conditions of rules against the current system state.

3. Conflict Resolution: If multiple rules are applicable, select one to apply.

4. Execute Action: Perform the action specified by the selected rule.

5. Update System State: Modify the system's state based on the action.

More Rules to Apply?: Check if additional rules are applicable.

- If yes, loop back to match conditions.
- If no, end the process.

Applications of Production Rules

Production rules are extensively used in various domains due to their flexibility and modularity. In expert systems, they encode domain knowledge for tasks like medical diagnosis, engineering troubleshooting, or legal decision-making. For example, the MYCIN expert system used production rules to diagnose bacterial infections and recommend treatments based on symptoms and lab results. In process control, production rules automate industrial operations by defining responses to specific conditions, such as releasing a valve if pressure exceeds a threshold.Production rules are also vital in decision support systems, where they analyze data to recommend actions. For example, in banking, production rules can evaluate customer profiles to decide credit approvals or loan eligibility.

Additionally, they are widely used in game AI to define the behavior of non-player characters (NPCs). For instance, a rule might state, "IF the player is within attack range, THEN attack," allowing NPCs to respond dynamically to player actions.

Advantages of Production Rules

One of the main advantages of production rules is their modularity. Each rule is a self-contained unit, making it easy to add, modify, or remove rules without affecting the rest of the system. This modularity simplifies the maintenance and scalability of rule-based systems. Production rules are also highly transparent; their IF-THEN structure is easy to understand, allowing domain experts to contribute to the rule base without needing extensive programming knowledge. Another strength is their flexibility, as production rules can handle complex logic by combining conditions with logical operators. This makes them suitable for a wide range of applications, from simple decision-making tasks to more complex reasoning processes. Furthermore, production rules enable automation, reducing the need for human intervention in repetitive or rule-based decision-making processes.

Introduction to Programming in Logic (PROLOG)

PROLOG (short for Programming in Logic) is a declarative programming language designed specifically for logic-based reasoning and symbolic computation. Developed in the early 1970s by Alain Colmerauer and his team, PROLOG is widely used in fields like artificial intelligence (AI), natural language processing, expert systems, and computational linguistics. Unlike procedural programming languages such as C++ or Python, PROLOG focuses on defining relationships and facts and allows the system to infer solutions through logical reasoning.

At its core, PROLOG relies on the principles of predicate logic and resolution. A PROLOG program consists of facts, rules, and queries. Facts represent known truths, rules define logical relationships between facts, and queries allow users to pose questions that the system resolves using its knowledge base. This structure makes PROLOG a natural fit for problems requiring complex reasoning, such as knowledge representation, expert systems, and automated theorem proving.

Concepts in PROLOG

Facts:

- Facts are basic assertions about the world that are assumed to be true.
- Example: parent(john, mary). means "John is the parent of Mary."

Rules:

- Rules define logical relationships between facts. They consist of a head (conclusion) and a body (conditions).

- Example: grandparent(X, Y) :- parent(X, Z), parent(Z, Y). means "X is a grandparent of Y if X is a parent of Z and Z is a parent of Y."

Queries:

- Queries are questions posed to the PROLOG interpreter to retrieve information or verify truths.

Example: ?- grandparent(john, X). asks, "Who is John a grandparent of?"

Backtracking:

- PROLOG uses backtracking to explore multiple possibilities when answering queries. It systematically searches through all potential solutions until the query is satisfied or all options are exhausted.

How PROLOG Works?

The execution of a PROLOG program involves a process of matching, inference, and backtracking. When a query is posed, the PROLOG interpreter attempts to match the query with facts and rules in the knowledge base. If the initial attempt fails, the interpreter backtracks to explore alternative paths until a solution is found or it concludes that no solution exists.

For example, consider the knowledge base:

parent(john, mary).

parent(mary, tom).

grandparent(X, Y) :- parent(X, Z), parent(Z, Y).

Querying ?- grandparent(john, tom). causes PROLOG to:

- Match grandparent(john, tom) to the rule grandparent(X, Y) :- parent(X, Z), parent(Z, Y).
- Substitute john for X and try to find Z such that parent(john, Z) holds.
- Find Z = mary and check if parent(mary, tom) is true.
- Confirm the query and return the result.

Applications of PROLOG

PROLOG finds extensive use in various domains due to its ability to reason logically and handle symbolic computation efficiently. In expert systems, PROLOG is used to encode domain-specific knowledge and provide reasoning capabilities, as seen in medical diagnosis systems like MYCIN, where it helps analyze symptoms and recommend treatments. In Natural Language Processing (NLP), PROLOG is employed to parse and interpret sentences, analyze grammar, and generate responses. For instance, grammar rules can be encoded in PROLOG to parse complex sentence structures. Another significant application is knowledge representation, where PROLOG represents intricate relationships and performs logical inference, such as modeling family trees or domain ontologies. In theorem proving, PROLOG automates mathematical proofs using logical inference techniques, demonstrating its utility in formal logic. Additionally, in robotics, PROLOG assists in planning sequences of actions based on specific goals and constraints, enabling robots to adapt and execute tasks effectively.

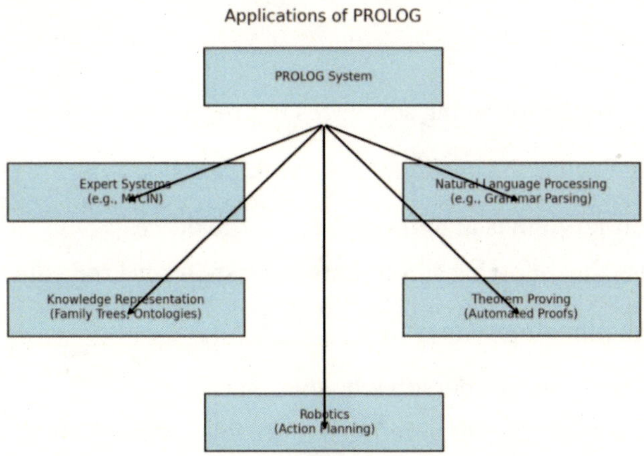

Advantages of PROLOG

PROLOG offers several advantages that make it a powerful tool for AI applications. Its declarative nature allows programmers to focus on what needs to be achieved rather than how to achieve it, simplifying the development process. The language provides built-in logical reasoning, enabling systems to perform inference without requiring extensive additional coding. PROLOG is highly expressive, making it ideal for problems that involve relationships, constraints, and symbolic computations. Furthermore, its backtracking mechanism systematically explores all possible solutions to ensure completeness, making it robust for solving complex problems.

Conclusion

Chapter 3 explores various techniques and frameworks for representing and reasoning about knowledge in artificial intelligence. It begins with Propositional Logic and First-Order Predicate Logic, foundational systems for expressing and inferring facts and relationships. The Resolution Principle and Unification are discussed as key mechanisms for logical inference. Semantic Nets, Conceptual Dependencies, and Frames and Scripts provide structured ways to model relationships, events, and stereotypical situations. Production Rules are introduced as a flexible method for encoding decision-making processes, while the chapter concludes with an introduction to PROLOG, a declarative programming language that leverages logical reasoning for applications like expert systems, natural language processing, and automated theorem proving. Together, these concepts form a comprehensive toolkit for knowledge representation and reasoning in AI. The next chapter delves into the components and processes involved in natural language communication, comparing formal and natural languages through grammar. It covers key topics like the Chomsky hierarchy, parsing techniques, semantics, and advanced grammar frameworks such as context-free and transformational grammars, as well as recursive and augmented transition networks.

Exercise:

- Represent the following sentences in propositional logic:
  - "If it rains, the ground will be wet."
  - "Either John is at home or he is at the office."
- Express the following statements in First-Order Predicate Logic:
  - "All humans are mortal."
  - "There exists a person who owns a car."
- Create a semantic net to represent the following relationships:
  - A dog is a mammal.
  - A dog has a tail and can bark.
- Represent the sentence "John gave Mary a book" using Conceptual Dependencies, including action, actor, object, and recipient.
- Design a frame to represent a "Car" with attributes like make, model, color, and owner.
- Develop a script for a "Grocery Shopping" scenario, including actions like entering the store, selecting items, and paying.
- Write production rules for a traffic light system:
  - Green light -> Allow cars to move.
  - Red light -> Stop cars.
- Write a simple PROLOG knowledge base for the following facts:
  - John is Mary's parent.
  - Mary is Tom's parent.
- Add a rule to define a grandparent relationship and query the system to find Tom's grandparent.

Discuss the advantages and limitations of using frames versus scripts in AI systems. Provide examples where each would be most appropriate.

4

Understanding Natural Languages

Introduction

This chapter explores the fundamentals of understanding natural languages, focusing on the components and steps involved in communication. It examines the differences between formal and natural languages, delves into grammar structures like the Chomsky hierarchy, and discusses parsing techniques, semantics, and advanced grammar frameworks.

Objective

The objective of this chapter is to provide a comprehensive understanding of natural language processing, including the mechanics of grammar, parsing methods, and semantic analysis. It aims to equip readers with knowledge of frameworks like context-free grammars and transition networks used in AI applications.

Components and Steps of Communication

Communication is the cornerstone of interaction, whether between humans or between humans and machines. It involves a systematic process where information is transmitted, received, and interpreted. Effective communication relies on several components and steps that work in harmony to ensure that the intended message reaches its recipient accurately. Understanding these elements is crucial in fields like artificial intelligence (AI), where systems are designed to simulate human communication.

Core Components of Communication

The communication process is driven by several key components. The sender is the originator of the message, responsible for formulating and encoding the information they wish to convey. The message itself represents the core idea or information being shared, while encoding converts this idea into a format suitable for transmission, such as spoken words, written text, or signals. The medium or channel is the pathway through which the message is transmitted, such as a phone call, email, or chatbot interface. The receiver is the target audience for the message, tasked with decoding and interpreting the information. Decoding involves extracting the intended meaning from the message, a process that requires shared understanding or context between sender and receiver. Finally, feedback completes the communication loop, as the receiver responds to the sender, confirming comprehension or seeking clarification. For example, in AI systems, feedback might be a user query or a command response.

Table: Components and Steps of Communication

Component/Step	Description	Example in AI
Sender	The originator of the message.	Virtual assistant like Siri formulating a response.
Message	The information or idea being conveyed.	A weather forecast or a recommendation.
Encoding	Converting the message into a suitable format for transmission.	NLP algorithms generating a text response.
Medium/Channel	The pathway for message transmission.	Voice commands or chatbot interface.
Receiver	The target audience of the message.	User interacting with the AI system.
Decoding	Interpreting and understanding the received message.	User interpreting the assistant's spoken or text reply.
Feedback	Response from the receiver indicating message comprehension.	User asking follow-up questions or performing actions.

Steps in the Communication Process

The communication process unfolds in distinct steps. It begins with idea formulation, where the sender develops the content and intent of the message. This is followed by message encoding, where the idea is translated into a communicable form. For instance, a virtual assistant encoding weather data into a spoken response is an example of this step. The message transmission step involves the delivery of the encoded message through the chosen channel, such as voice or text. The next step, message reception, occurs when the receiver perceives the transmitted information, such as a user reading a chatbot response. The decoding process follows, where the receiver interprets the content and extracts its meaning. The final step, feedback, ensures that the sender knows whether the message was understood. This step is crucial in both human and machine communication, as it allows for clarification or follow-up actions.

Challenges in Communication

Despite the structured nature of communication, several challenges can disrupt the process. Noise refers to any interference that distorts the message during transmission. In human communication, noise might include background sounds, while in AI systems, it could be signal loss or data corruption. Ambiguity is another challenge, where messages are open to multiple interpretations, potentially leading to misunderstandings. AI systems often struggle with ambiguous language and rely on context or training data to resolve such issues. Medium limitations can also hinder communication, as the chosen channel may not fully convey the nuances of the message, such as emotions in text-based interactions.

Relevance to AI Systems

Understanding the components and steps of communication is integral to the design of AI systems like chatbots, virtual assistants, and automated translators. For example, a virtual assistant like Alexa acts as the sender when responding to user queries. Natural Language Processing (NLP) algorithms handle the encoding and decoding processes, while the user serves as the receiver. Feedback occurs when the user provides further input or performs an action based on the assistant's response. By modeling human communication processes, AI systems aim to achieve clarity, accuracy, and a natural interaction flow.

The Contrast between Formal and Natural Languages in the Context of Grammar

The contrast between formal and natural languages in the context of grammar highlights the fundamental differences in their structure, purpose, and usage. Grammar, as a system of rules governing the composition of words, phrases, and sentences, takes on distinct roles in these two domains. Formal languages, such as programming or mathematical languages, and natural languages, like English or Mandarin, differ significantly in terms of ambiguity, flexibility, precision, and evolution.

The figure provides a comparative visualization of key characteristics between formal and natural languages in the context of grammar. It highlights that ambiguity is significantly higher in natural languages due to their nuanced and context-dependent meanings, whereas formal languages are designed to avoid ambiguity entirely. Flexibility is another domain where natural languages excel, allowing for creativity and evolution, unlike the rigid structure of formal languages. In contrast, precision is a defining feature of formal languages, ensuring clarity and exactness, which natural languages often sacrifice for expressiveness. Lastly, the rate of evolution is rapid in natural languages, adapting organically to cultural and societal shifts, whereas formal languages evolve slowly and deliberately to maintain consistency and reliability.

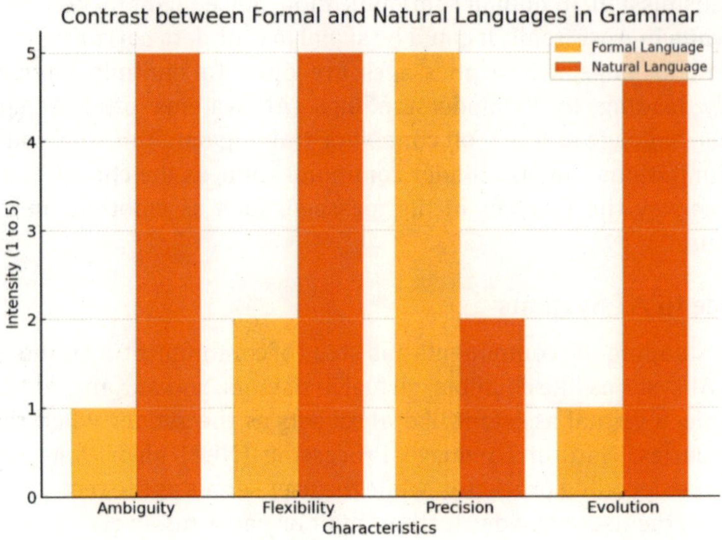

Ambiguity

One of the most striking differences lies in ambiguity. Natural languages are inherently ambiguous, with words and sentences often possessing multiple meanings. This ambiguity allows for richness and depth, enabling nuanced expression, cultural references, and figurative language. For example, "I saw her duck" could mean observing someone crouch or spotting their waterfowl. On the other hand, formal languages are designed to eliminate ambiguity entirely. Every statement in a formal language has a precise, unambiguous meaning defined by its syntax and semantics, ensuring clarity in contexts like programming or logic.

Flexibility

Flexibility is another area where natural and formal languages diverge. Natural languages evolve dynamically and permit creativity, with speakers often breaking grammatical rules for stylistic or rhetorical purposes. Slang, idiomatic expressions, and evolving cultural contexts all contribute to this flexibility. Formal languages, however, are rigid by necessity. They adhere strictly to predefined rules, as deviations could result in misinterpretation or errors, especially in fields like computer programming or mathematical proofs.

Precision

Formal languages prioritize precision. Their grammar is explicitly designed to convey exact instructions or information, making them indispensable in fields where accuracy is paramount. In contrast, natural languages often trade precision for expressiveness and contextual depth. While natural language allows for vague or open-ended communication that relies on shared understanding and context, formal languages depend on their strict grammar to avoid miscommunication entirely.

Evolution

The evolution of natural and formal languages also reflects their fundamental differences. Natural languages change continuously over time, influenced by cultural, technological, and social factors. Words emerge, shift meanings, or fade into obscurity, and grammatical structures adapt to meet the needs of speakers. Formal languages, however, are intentionally stable. Changes occur infrequently and only through deliberate updates or revisions by governing bodies, ensuring consistency across users and applications.

Purpose and Audience

The ultimate purpose of each language type further underscores their differences. Natural languages aim to facilitate human interaction, conveying emotions, ideas, and cultural identity. Their grammar evolves to meet the diverse needs of speakers across different contexts. Formal languages, however, are tools for precision communication in technical domains. Their grammar is designed to be strictly logical and universally interpretable by humans and machines, serving a specific functional purpose rather than an expressive one.

Chomsky Hierarchy of Grammars

The Chomsky Hierarchy, proposed by Noam Chomsky in 1956, is a classification of formal grammars that generate languages, which are sets of strings over a given alphabet. It organizes these grammars into four levels based on their generative power and the computational resources required to process them. Each level of the hierarchy encompasses a broader range of grammars and languages than the level below it.

Type 0: Unrestricted Grammars

Unrestricted grammars, also known as Type 0 grammars, represent the most general form of formal grammars in the Chomsky hierarchy. These grammars impose no restrictions on their production rules, which are expressed in the form $\alpha \to \beta$, where α and β are strings of terminals and non-terminals, and α must include at least one non-terminal. Because of this generality, Type 0 grammars can express any computable function or algorithm. The languages generated by unrestricted grammars are known as recursively enumerable languages, meaning they can be recognized by a Turing machine. These grammars are immensely powerful but lack practical utility in most applications due to their complexity and the undecidability of many properties, such as determining whether a given string belongs to the language. Unrestricted grammars are primarily studied in theoretical computer science to understand the limits of computation and language expressiveness.

Type 1: Context-Sensitive Grammars (CSG)

Context-sensitive grammars (CSG), or Type 1 grammars, are a subset of unrestricted grammars that introduce a key restriction: the length of the string on the right-hand side (β) must be greater than or equal to the length of the string on the left-hand side (α). This restriction ensures that the rules preserve or increase the length of the string, making these grammars context-sensitive. The production rules are expressed as $\alpha A\beta \rightarrow \alpha\gamma\beta$, where A is a non-terminal, and α,

β, and γ are strings of terminals and non-terminals.Context-sensitive grammars generate context-sensitive languages, which are recognized by a linear-bounded automaton, a type of Turing machine with memory bounded by the size of the input string. These grammars are powerful enough to describe languages with dependencies on the surrounding context, such as agreements in natural languages (e.g., subject-verb agreement). Despite their expressive power, they are less commonly used due to their computational complexity.

Type 2: Context-Free Grammars (CFG)

Context-free grammars (CFG), or Type 2 grammars, are simpler and more restricted than context-sensitive grammars. The production rules in a CFG must have a single non-terminal on the left-hand side (A) and any string of terminals and non-terminals on the right-hand side (γ), expressed as $A \rightarrow \gamma$. This simplicity makes CFGs easier to parse and implement, which is why they are extensively used in computer science and linguistics.CFGs generate context-free languages, which are recognized by a pushdown automaton, a computational model that uses a stack for memory. These languages can describe structures with nested dependencies, such as balanced parentheses or nested loops in programming languages. As a result, CFGs form the backbone of many applications, including programming language syntax, compilers, and natural language processing.

Type 3: Regular Grammars

Regular grammars, or Type 3 grammars, are the most restricted and simplest form of grammars in the Chomsky hierarchy. Their production rules are limited to two forms:

A→aB and A→a, where A and B are non-terminals, and a is a terminal. This strict structure ensures that the languages generated by regular grammars are straightforward and finite in their complexity. Regular grammars generate regular languages, which are recognized by a finite automaton, a computational model with limited memory that processes input sequentially. These languages are widely used for describing simple patterns, such as regular expressions in text processing or patterns in lexical analysis. Regular grammars are prevalent in applications like tokenization in programming languages, pattern matching, and text search engines due to their simplicity and efficiency.

Relationship Between the Types

The Chomsky hierarchy is inclusive, with each type of grammar being a subset of the more general types above it. Regular grammars (Type 3) are a subset of context-free grammars (Type 2), which are themselves a subset of context-sensitive grammars (Type 1). Finally, context-sensitive grammars are a subset of unrestricted grammars (Type 0). This nested structure reflects the increasing generality and computational power as you move up the hierarchy. Each type of grammar serves specific theoretical and practical purposes, making the Chomsky hierarchy a foundational concept in formal language theory and computational linguistics.

Parsing, and Semantics

Parsing: The Process of Analyzing Language Structure

Parsing refers to the process of analyzing a string of symbols (typically a sentence or code) according to the rules of a grammar. It is a fundamental operation in both natural and formal languages, enabling machines and humans to understand the structure and relationships within a given input. Parsing breaks down complex inputs into smaller, more manageable components, often represented in a hierarchical structure called a parse tree or syntax tree. In the context of programming languages, parsing is an essential step in the compilation or interpretation process. The parser uses a grammar, often defined in a formal language, to validate the syntax of the input code and build a structured representation. For example, in a programming language, parsing ensures that expressions like x + y follow the rules for valid operator usage and operand placement. Similarly, in natural language processing (NLP), parsing analyzes sentences to identify their grammatical components, such as subjects, verbs, and objects, and their relationships.

Parsing typically involves two phases: lexical analysis and syntactic analysis. Lexical analysis identifies tokens (basic units like keywords or symbols), while syntactic analysis checks the sequence of tokens against the rules of the grammar. The output of parsing serves as a foundation for further processing, such as semantic interpretation or code generation.

Semantics: Understanding Meaning

Semantics deals with the meaning of linguistic or symbolic expressions, going beyond the structural analysis provided by parsing. While parsing focuses on verifying the structure of a sentence or code, semantics ensures that the content is meaningful within a given context or domain. In essence, semantics interprets the "what" behind the "how" of a statement. In programming languages, semantics ensures that operations are meaningful and consistent with the intended functionality. For example, the expression 5 / 0 may be syntactically valid but semantically meaningless because division by zero is undefined. Semantic analysis often involves type checking, ensuring that variables, functions, and operators are used correctly. For instance, trying to add a string and a number might pass parsing but fail semantic checks in many programming languages. In natural languages, semantics addresses the meanings of words, phrases, and sentences. It encompasses tasks like resolving ambiguities, understanding metaphors, and interpreting context. For example, the word "bank" might refer to a financial institution or the side of a river, depending on the sentence. Semantic analysis in NLP uses techniques like semantic networks, embeddings, and ontologies to model and interpret meaning.

Parsing and Semantics: Interplay and Applications

Parsing and semantics are complementary processes. Parsing establishes a foundation by identifying valid structures, while semantics builds on that foundation to derive meaning. Together, they enable machines to process and understand both human and formal languages effectively. In programming, parsing ensures that code adheres to syntax rules, and semantic analysis checks for logical correctness. This combination is crucial for creating reliable compilers and interpreters. In NLP, parsing extracts grammatical relationships, and semantics interprets the intent, enabling applications like machine translation, chatbots, and question-answering systems. Both processes are integral to bridging the gap between raw input (code or text) and actionable understanding, forming the backbone of computational linguistics and modern software development.

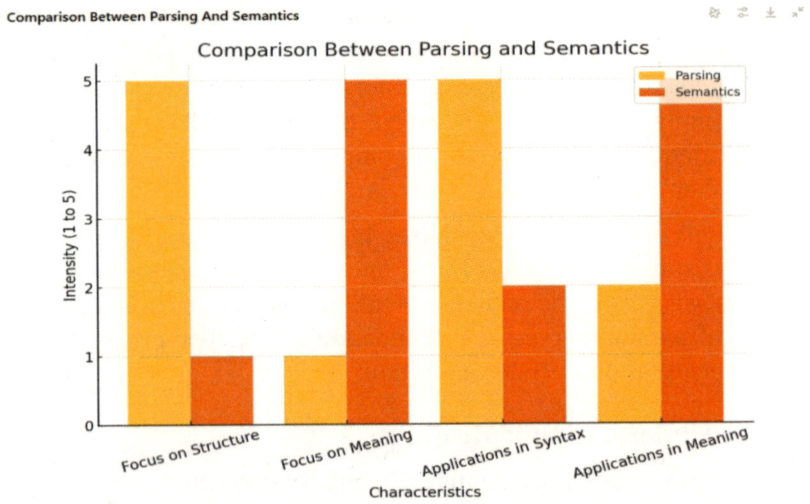

The figure visually compares parsing and semantics across four key characteristics: focus on structure, focus on meaning, applications in syntax, and applications in meaning. Parsing dominates in areas requiring structural analysis and syntax validation, represented by higher scores in "Focus on Structure" and "Applications in Syntax." In contrast, semantics excels in interpreting and assigning meaning, as seen in higher scores for "Focus on Meaning" and "Applications in

Meaning." This comparison highlights the complementary roles of parsing and semantics, where parsing ensures structural validity, and semantics provides contextual understanding. Together, they enable comprehensive language processing.

Parsing Techniques

Parsing techniques refer to the methods used to analyze the syntax of a string according to a grammar. These techniques play a vital role in various applications, including programming language compilers, interpreters, and natural language processing (NLP) systems. Parsing techniques can be broadly categorized into top-down parsing and bottom-up parsing, with further variations within each category.

1.Top-Down Parsing

Top-down parsing is a parsing technique that begins with the start symbol of a grammar and attempts to derive the input string by applying production rules. This method constructs the parse tree from the root downward to the leaves, following the grammar's rules. It is intuitive and works well for simple grammars, but it has limitations in handling complex or ambiguous structures.

a) Recursive Descent Parsing

Recursive descent parsing is a straightforward implementation of top-down parsing where each non-terminal in the grammar is represented by a recursive procedure. The parser attempts to match the input string with the production rules by recursively expanding non-terminals. While simple to implement, this technique struggles with grammars that include left recursion, as it leads to infinite recursion. For example, a grammar with the rule $A \rightarrow A\alpha$ would cause the parser to loop indefinitely. Despite its limitations, recursive descent parsing is widely used for small, manually designed grammars, particularly in educational settings or for simple domain-specific languages. Developers often address left recursion by rewriting the grammar or adopting predictive parsing techniques.

b) Predictive Parsing

Predictive parsing refines recursive descent parsing by using a lookahead symbol to decide which production rule to apply. This technique avoids backtracking, making parsing more efficient. To achieve this, the grammar must be an LL(1) grammar, which means it allows left-to-right scanning of the input and leftmost derivation with a single lookahead symbol. While predictive parsing eliminates some limitations of recursive descent parsing, it requires grammar transformation to remove left recursion and factor out common prefixes.

2. Bottom-Up Parsing

Bottom-up parsing constructs the parse tree by starting from the input string's leaves and working backward toward the root (start symbol). This technique is more powerful than top-down parsing, as it can handle a wider range of grammars, including ambiguous and left-recursive grammars. It focuses on reducing substrings of the input string into non-terminals based on grammar rules.

a) Shift-Reduce Parsing

Shift-reduce parsing is a common bottom-up parsing method that uses a stack to hold grammar components. The parser performs two primary operations: shift, which pushes the next input symbol onto the stack, and reduce, which replaces a sequence of symbols on the stack with the corresponding non-terminal. The process continues until the stack contains only the start symbol. Shift-reduce parsing is efficient for simple grammars but can face conflicts in ambiguous grammars, such as deciding between shift and reduce actions. These conflicts are resolved using advanced strategies or by modifying the grammar.

b) LR Parsing

LR parsing (Left-to-right scanning with Rightmost derivation in reverse) is the most robust bottom-up parsing method. It is suitable for a wide range of context-free grammars, including those used in programming languages. LR parsers use a parsing table to guide the shift and reduce operations, making them deterministic and efficient.

There are several variants of LR parsing:

- SLR (Simple LR): Simplifies table construction but has limited power.
- Canonical LR: Handles the full range of LR grammars but requires large tables.
- LALR (Lookahead LR): Balances power and efficiency by merging similar states in Canonical LR, making it widely used in practice.
- LR parsing is computationally intensive to implement manually but is highly effective for large-scale applications like compiler construction.

3. Advanced Parsing Techniques

Advanced parsing techniques are designed to handle more complex grammars and situations where traditional top-down or bottom-up methods fall short. These techniques are particularly useful in scenarios involving ambiguous grammars or non-standard structures.

a) CYK (Cocke-Younger-Kasami) Algorithm

The CYK algorithm is a dynamic programming approach used to parse context-free grammars in Chomsky Normal Form (CNF). It breaks the input string into substrings and systematically combines them to form higher-level constructs. The algorithm ensures that all possible parse trees are considered, making it suitable for ambiguous grammars. Despite its versatility, the CYK algorithm has a computational complexity of $O(n3)$, where n is the length of the input string. This makes it less practical for real-time applications but valuable in theoretical studies and NLP tasks where all possible parses are required.

b) Earley Parser

The Earley parser is a general-purpose algorithm for parsing all context-free grammars, including those with left recursion. It works efficiently for unambiguous grammars and can produce a parse tree or multiple trees for ambiguous inputs. The algorithm uses a dynamic approach to process the input incrementally, making it suitable for real-time and streaming applications. The Earley parser is more flexible than CYK and other methods, but it can be slower for highly ambiguous grammars. It is particularly useful in natural language processing, where grammatical structures are often complex and ambiguous.

4. Comparison of Parsing Techniques

Top-down and bottom-up parsing differ significantly in their approach and capabilities. Top-down parsing starts from the grammar's start symbol and attempts to match the input, while bottom-up parsing begins with the input and builds toward the start symbol. Top-down methods, such as recursive descent and predictive parsing, are intuitive and simpler to implement but are limited to specific types of grammars like LL(1). In contrast, bottom-up methods like shift-reduce and LR parsing are more powerful, capable of handling left-recursive and ambiguous grammars. LR parsing, in particular, is widely used in programming language compilers due to its efficiency and robustness. Advanced techniques like CYK and Earley parsing address even more complex scenarios, though they come with higher computational costs.

5. Applications of Parsing Techniques

Parsing techniques are indispensable in various domains. In compilers and interpreters, parsing validates syntax and constructs parse trees, which serve as the basis for code generation and optimization. In natural language processing, parsing enables grammatical analysis, aiding tasks like machine translation, sentiment analysis, and question answering. Query processing in databases relies on parsing to validate and optimize SQL queries before execution. Additionally, parsing is integral to code editors and integrated development environments (IDEs), providing features like real-time syntax highlighting, error checking, and code suggestions. The choice of parsing technique depends on the complexity of the grammar and the application's performance requirements, underscoring the versatility and importance of parsing in modern computing.

Different parsing techniques, including their approach, advantages, disadvantages, and applications

Parsing Technique	Approach	Advantages	Disadvantages	Applications
Recursive Descent Parsing	Top-Down	Simple implementation, intuitive for small grammars	Cannot handle left-recursive grammars, limited to simple cases	Simple parsers, educational tools
Predictive Parsing	Top-Down	Efficient without backtracking, suitable for LL(1) grammars	Limited to LL(1) grammars, requires grammar transformation	Small domain-specific languages, predictable grammars
Shift-Reduce Parsing	Bottom-Up	Handles left-recursive grammars, simple parsing strategy	Ambiguity resolution can be challenging, limited by stack-based approach	Basic compilers, syntax analysis
LR Parsing (SLR, Canonical LR, LALR)	Bottom-Up	Efficient and robust for programming languages	Complex implementation, requires table generation	Programming language compilers, advanced syntax validation
CYK Algorithm	Dynamic Programming	Handles all context-free grammars, finds all parse trees	Computationally intensive (O(n^3)), suitable for theoretical use	Theoretical studies, natural language processing
Earley Parser	Dynamic Programming	General-purpose, handles left recursion and ambiguity	Can be slower for highly ambiguous grammars	Real-time NLP tasks, ambiguous grammar handling

Context-Free and Transformational Grammars

Context-Free Grammars (CFG)

Context-Free Grammars (CFG) are a type of formal grammar used to define the syntax of programming languages and model the structural aspects of natural languages. CFGs are characterized by production rules where a single non-terminal symbol on the left-hand side is replaced by a sequence of terminal and/or non-terminal symbols on the right-hand side. This structure allows CFGs to handle hierarchical and recursive patterns, such as nested parentheses or complex sentence structures. For example, the grammar rule $S \to (S) \mid \epsilon$ can generate balanced parentheses, illustrating the ability of CFGs to describe nested dependencies. CFGs are widely used in computer science for applications such as designing programming languages, building parsers for compilers, and creating syntax analyzers. They are also foundational in natural language processing (NLP) for syntactic analysis, helping to parse sentences into grammatical components like subjects and predicates. However, CFGs have limitations, as they cannot model context-sensitive dependencies, such as subject-verb agreement in natural languages, where the choice of one word depends on another's grammatical role.

Transformational Grammars

Transformational Grammars were introduced by Noam Chomsky to go beyond the limitations of simpler grammars, such as CFGs, in capturing the complexities of natural language. This model differentiates between the deep structure, which represents the abstract meaning of a sentence, and the surface structure, which corresponds to the actual spoken or written form. Transformations, such as moving words or phrases, connect these structures, making it possible to explain linguistic phenomena like passive constructions or question formation. For instance, the transformation from "The boy is running" to "Is the boy running?" involves rearranging elements while retaining the same core meaning. This grammar system allows for a richer understanding of language by incorporating context-sensitive rules and handling variations in sentence structure. It has been instrumental in linguistic theory, providing insights into universal grammar and the processes underlying language acquisition. Transformational grammars also find applications in NLP tasks that require deep syntactic and semantic analysis, such as machine translation or dialogue systems, where surface-level processing alone is insufficient.

Comparison of CFG and Transformational Grammars

While both CFGs and transformational grammars are tools for modeling language, they differ significantly in focus and scope. CFGs emphasize syntactic structure through simple production rules, making them suitable for defining programming language syntax and basic NLP tasks. They excel in describing hierarchical relationships but are limited in handling context-sensitive dependencies. In contrast, transformational grammars delve deeper into the relationship between meaning and structure by distinguishing between deep and surface structures. They use transformational rules to account for complex linguistic phenomena, making them more powerful but also more computationally intensive. CFGs are easier to implement and are widely used in practical applications like compiler design, where speed and simplicity are critical. On the other hand, transformational grammars offer theoretical insights into language and are better suited for advanced NLP and linguistic studies. Their ability to model intricate grammatical rules and transformations makes them valuable in fields that require a nuanced understanding of language, such as artificial intelligence and cognitive science.

Applications of CFGs and Transformational Grammars

CFGs are integral to fields like programming language development and syntax analysis. They provide a clear and efficient framework for defining the grammatical structure of code, ensuring that programs are syntactically valid. In NLP, CFGs help analyze sentence structure, enabling tasks like sentence parsing and grammar checking. Transformational grammars, however, shine in more complex linguistic applications. They are crucial in understanding and modeling natural languages, handling context-sensitive rules, and transforming abstract representations into natural-sounding sentences. Transformational grammars have broader implications in linguistic theory, where they provide a framework for exploring how humans produce and understand language. They also support advanced NLP applications like machine translation and sentiment analysis, where the relationship between syntax and meaning is critical. Together, these grammars address both the structural and transformational aspects of language, highlighting their complementary roles in computational linguistics and artificial intelligence.

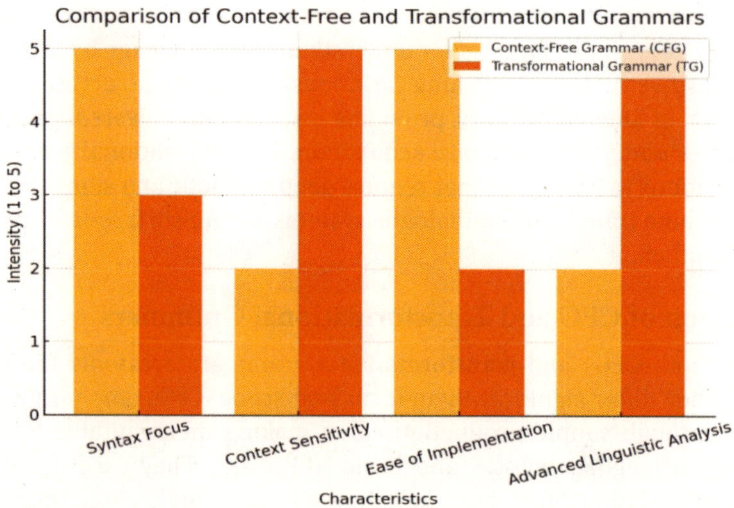

The figure illustrates a comparison between Context-Free Grammars (CFG) and Transformational Grammars (TG) across four key characteristics: syntax focus, context sensitivity, ease of implementation, and advanced linguistic analysis. CFGs excel in syntax focus and ease of implementation, making them suitable for tasks like programming language syntax analysis. On the other hand, Transformational Grammars outperform in context sensitivity and advanced linguistic analysis, highlighting their capability to model complex language phenomena and deeper structural relationships. This visualization underscores their complementary strengths in language modeling.

Recursive and Augmented Transition Nets

Recursive Transition Networks (RTNs)

Recursive Transition Networks (RTNs) are a formalism used to represent the syntax of languages in a graphical manner. They extend the concept of finite-state automata by allowing recursion, which makes them particularly useful for modeling context-free grammars. In RTNs, states are represented as nodes, and transitions between states are represented as directed edges. These transitions can point to other sub-networks, enabling recursion and hierarchical representations.RTNs are widely used in natural language processing (NLP) to model syntactic structures, especially for languages with nested or recursive patterns. For example, the sentence "The cat that the dog chased ran away" involves embedding clauses, which RTNs can effectively represent by allowing states to call other sub-networks recursively. This makes RTNs more expressive than simple finite-state automata.

A key advantage of RTNs is their visual clarity, which allows linguists and computer scientists to intuitively understand and design grammars. However, they are limited in handling context-sensitive dependencies, such as agreement between words, where additional mechanisms or extensions are required.

Augmented Transition Networks (ATNs)

Augmented Transition Networks (ATNs) are an enhancement of RTNs that incorporate additional features like registers and procedural actions. These augmentations enable ATNs to handle more complex language phenomena, including context-sensitive dependencies, by performing computations or storing intermediate results during transitions. Registers are variables that can hold information, such as the subject of a sentence, which can later be used to resolve agreement or other relationships.ATNs are particularly powerful for parsing natural languages, as they combine the hierarchical representation of RTNs with the computational capabilities of procedural programming. For instance, an ATN can parse a sentence like "The boy who saw the girl smiled" by storing the subject ("The boy") in a register and using this information to ensure grammatical correctness in the remainder of the sentence.One of the significant advantages of ATNs is their flexibility. They can parse ambiguous and complex sentences by storing and managing different interpretations simultaneously. However, this added complexity comes at a computational cost, making ATNs slower and more resource-intensive compared to simpler models.

Differences Between RTNs and ATNs

While both RTNs and ATNs are graphical models for representing grammars, their capabilities differ significantly. RTNs are limited to context-free grammars and rely on recursive calls to represent hierarchical structures. In contrast, ATNs extend this framework with procedural actions and registers, making them capable of modeling context-sensitive languages and handling more complex linguistic phenomena.ATNs are particularly suitable for natural language processing tasks where syntactic structures interact with semantic or contextual information. They are more expressive but also more computationally demanding. RTNs, on the other hand, are simpler and more efficient for tasks that do not require context-sensitive analysis.

Applications of RTNs and ATNs

RTNs and ATNs have been widely applied in computational linguistics and NLP. RTNs are used for syntax analysis and parsing tasks where context-free grammars are sufficient, such as identifying parts of speech or basic sentence structures. They are also helpful in educational tools for teaching the basics of formal language theory.ATNs are used in advanced NLP applications, such as machine translation, speech recognition, and dialogue systems. Their ability to store contextual information and handle ambiguity makes them valuable for parsing complex sentences, understanding language nuances, and generating meaningful responses in conversational AI systems.

Advantages and Limitations

Both RTNs and ATNs offer unique advantages and face specific limitations. RTNs are simple, efficient, and easy to visualize, making them suitable for a wide range of applications. However, their inability to handle context-sensitive dependencies limits their use in natural language parsing. ATNs overcome this limitation by incorporating computational capabilities, but they are more complex to design and implement. Choosing between RTNs and ATNs depends on the complexity of the language being modeled and the computational resources available. For simple, structured tasks, RTNs are often sufficient, while ATNs are more suitable for handling the intricacies of natural language.

Comparison Table: RTNs vs. ATNs

Aspect	Recursive Transition Networks (RTNs)	Augmented Transition Networks (ATNs)
Grammar Representation	Context-Free	Context-Sensitive
Mechanism	Recursive calls to sub-networks	Registers and procedural actions
Expressiveness	Limited to syntax	Handles syntax and context-sensitive semantics
Applications	Syntax analysis, simple parsing tasks	Advanced NLP, machine translation, speech systems
Advantages	Simple, efficient, easy to visualize	Flexible, handles ambiguity, stores context
Limitations	Cannot handle context-sensitive dependencies	Computationally intensive, more complex

This table summarizes the differences between RTNs and ATNs, highlighting their strengths, limitations, and suitable applications.

Conclusion

This chapter explores the key components and steps of communication, highlighting the differences between formal and natural languages in grammar. It covers the Chomsky hierarchy of grammars, parsing and semantics, parsing techniques, and the distinctions between context-free and transformational grammars. Finally, it examines Recursive and Augmented Transition Nets, emphasizing their roles in syntax representation and natural language processing. Next chapter delves into the evolution of AI, contrasting symbolic AI with data-driven approaches like machine learning and deep learning. It explores applications of both paradigms, introduces interpretable and explainable AI, and discusses the ethical implications, benefits, and risks of AI in shaping the future.

Exercise:

- Describe the key components and steps involved in effective communication. Provide examples to illustrate each step.
- Compare and contrast formal and natural languages in terms of grammar, ambiguity, flexibility, and precision. How do these differences impact their applications?
- Explain the Chomsky hierarchy of grammars and provide examples for each type of grammar (Type 0 to Type 3). Why is this hierarchy important in understanding language processing?

- Define parsing and semantics in the context of language processing. How do they complement each other in understanding natural and formal languages?
- Discuss the differences between top-down and bottom-up parsing techniques. Provide examples of where each technique might be more suitable.
- Write a context-free grammar for a language that generates balanced parentheses and provide a parse tree for the string ((())).
- Explain the concepts of deep structure and surface structure in transformational grammars. How do transformational rules bridge the two?
- Draw a Recursive Transition Network (RTN) for simple sentences with embedded clauses, such as "The cat that chased the mouse ran away."
- Explain how Augmented Transition Networks (ATNs) extend the capabilities of RTNs. Provide an example of how ATNs handle context-sensitive dependencies.
- Discuss two applications of parsing techniques and grammars in natural language processing. How do these techniques enable machines to understand human language?

5

AI the Present and the Future

Introduction

Artificial Intelligence (AI) is transforming industries and society by enabling machines to perform tasks that traditionally required human intelligence. This chapter delves into the evolution of AI, covering foundational paradigms such as Symbolic AI and Data-driven AI, alongside modern advancements like Machine Learning and Explainable AI. By examining AI's applications, ethical considerations, and its benefits and risks, the chapter provides a holistic view of its current impact and future potential.

Objective

The objective of this chapter is to explore the key methodologies, applications, and ethical challenges of AI, highlighting its transformative role in the present and future. It aims to equip readers with a deeper understanding of AI's potential, limitations, and the importance of developing and deploying it responsibly to benefit humanity.

Artificial Intelligence (AI) is reshaping the present across industries, from healthcare and finance to entertainment and transportation. Its ability to process vast amounts of data, identify patterns, and make decisions has enabled advancements like personalized medicine, fraud detection, self-driving cars, and conversational agents. AI is also revolutionizing creative fields, allowing for the generation of art, music, and content. At the core, AI combines machine learning, natural language processing, and computer vision to mimic human intelligence, offering both efficiency and innovation. Yet, it also raises ethical concerns, such as biases in decision-making, job displacement, and privacy issues. The future of AI holds even greater potential and complexity. Advances in quantum computing, neural networks, and general AI aim to create systems with reasoning capabilities closer to human cognition. Applications like advanced robotics, human-computer brain interfaces, and predictive analytics could transform sectors like space exploration, education, and governance. However, with these opportunities come challenges: ensuring ethical development, mitigating the risk of misuse, and establishing robust regulations to guide AI's evolution responsibly. The trajectory of AI promises profound benefits but requires a balance of innovation, ethical oversight, and societal preparedness.

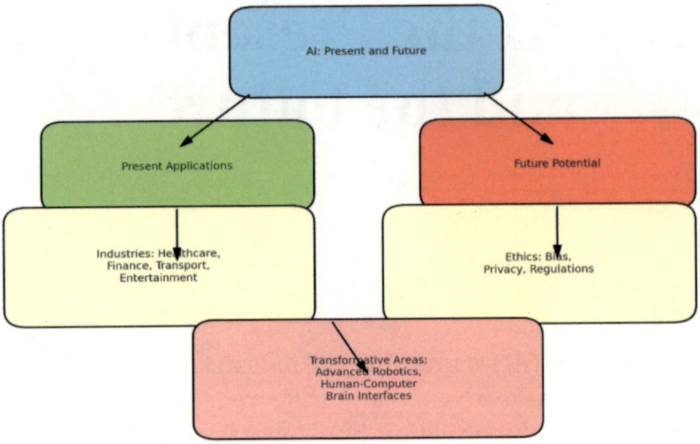

Figure 5.1: Present and Future of AI.

The flowchart illustrates the relationship between AI's present applications and its future potential (Figure 5.1). It highlights current domains like healthcare and finance under "Present Applications" and ethical considerations under "Future Potential," leading to transformative advancements such as advanced robotics and brain-computer interfaces. The arrows depict the progression of AI's influence and impact.

Symbolic AI

What is Symbolic AI?

Symbolic AI, also known as "Good Old-Fashioned Artificial Intelligence" (GOFAI), is a branch of artificial intelligence that relies on high-level, human-readable symbols and rules to represent knowledge and reasoning. Developed in the mid-20th century, Symbolic AI aims to mimic human cognition by encoding information in a structured and logical format, enabling machines to perform problem-solving, planning, and decision-making tasks.

1. Representation of Knowledge

Symbolic AI relies on structured knowledge representation using symbols, relationships, and hierarchies. Entities in the real world are abstracted into symbols (e.g., "Dog," "Tree"), and their attributes or relationships are encoded explicitly. For example, a knowledge base might represent a dog as an entity with properties like "has four legs" and "barks." This structured format makes the information understandable by humans and machines alike. This explicit encoding allows symbolic AI systems to store facts, concepts, and their interconnections in logical databases or ontologies. Examples include semantic networks and frames, where nodes represent concepts, and edges represent relationships. Such representations enable reasoning systems to infer new facts by combining existing information. However, these systems require manual curation, which can be time-intensive.

2. Logic and Rules

Symbolic AI employs formal logic, such as propositional and predicate logic, to reason about the information stored in its knowledge base. Logical expressions like "IF-THEN" rules are used to derive conclusions. For instance, a rule might state, "If an animal is a dog, it is a mammal," enabling the system to deduce new facts by chaining rules together. The use of logic provides high accuracy and ensures deterministic behavior, as every outcome is derived from pre-defined rules. However, this rigidity makes it difficult for symbolic AI to handle incomplete or ambiguous information, unlike probabilistic systems like machine learning. Despite this limitation, the precision of logical reasoning is invaluable in applications requiring strict accuracy and explainability.

3. Search and Planning

Symbolic AI uses search algorithms to explore possible solutions in a problem space. These include strategies like breadth-first search, depth-first search, and heuristic-based approaches. For example, in solving a maze, the system evaluates different paths using these techniques to find the optimal solution. Planning involves breaking down a goal into smaller, manageable sub-goals and finding a sequence of actions to achieve them. Symbolic planners like STRIPS (Stanford Research Institute Problem Solver) use logical representations to model the initial state, goal state, and actions. This capability has been widely used in robotics, logistics, and automated scheduling.

4. Explainability

One of Symbolic AI's greatest strengths is its interpretability. Since its operations are rule-based and deterministic, every decision made by the system can be traced back to the underlying rules and knowledge. For instance, an expert system diagnosing a disease can explicitly show the reasoning process, like "Symptom A + Symptom B = Disease X." This transparency makes Symbolic AI suitable for critical applications such as healthcare, legal decision-making, and finance, where understanding the reasoning behind a conclusion is essential. Unlike modern machine learning models, which often function as "black boxes," symbolic AI aligns closely with ethical standards requiring explainable outputs.

5. Applications of Symbolic AI

Symbolic AI has been employed in various domains:

- Expert Systems: Systems like MYCIN (for medical diagnosis) and DENDRAL (for chemical analysis) use encoded expert knowledge to make decisions and offer recommendations. These systems excel in niche fields where expertise can be codified into rules.
- Natural Language Understanding: Early NLP systems used symbolic AI to parse sentences, identify grammatical structures, and understand meaning. These systems relied on handcrafted rules and grammars.
- Robotics: Symbolic AI is used for task planning in robots, allowing them to perform structured actions like assembling products or navigating predefined paths.
- Game Playing: Systems like IBM's Deep Blue used symbolic reasoning to analyze potential moves and strategies, ultimately defeating human chess champions.

Table 5.1: Overview of Symbolic AI.

Aspect	Description	Examples
Knowledge Representation	Symbols and logical relationships to encode facts and entities.	Semantic networks, frames, ontologies
Logic and Rules	Formal logic systems used to derive conclusions through reasoning.	Propositional logic, predicate logic
Search and Planning	Algorithms to explore solutions and plan sequences of actions.	STRIPS, heuristic search
Explainability	Transparent and interpretable decision-making processes.	Diagnosis in expert systems, reasoning in legal applications
Applications	Niche domains where explicit knowledge is essential.	MYCIN, DENDRAL, Deep Blue
Challenges	Scalability, adaptability, and inability to handle ambiguous or incomplete data.	Difficulty scaling to large domains or integrating with real-world noisy data
Future Potential	Hybrid systems combining symbolic reasoning with machine learning to address current limitations.	Neuro-symbolic AI, explainable AI (XAI)

This comprehensive breakdown captures the depth and breadth of Symbolic AI's methodologies, strengths, and challenges (Table 5.1).

6. Challenges of Symbolic AI

Despite its strengths, Symbolic AI faces significant challenges:

- Scalability: As the scope of a domain increases, encoding all necessary knowledge and rules becomes infeasible. Updating the knowledge base to reflect new discoveries requires extensive manual effort.

- Adaptability: Symbolic systems struggle with learning from new data or adapting to unforeseen scenarios. Unlike machine learning, which can generalize from examples, symbolic AI requires explicit programming for every eventuality.
- Ambiguity in Real-World Data: The structured and deterministic nature of Symbolic AI makes it ill-suited to handle noisy or incomplete data, limiting its applicability in dynamic environments.

Data-driven AI and Machine Learning

Data-Driven AI

Data-driven AI relies on extracting patterns, insights, and predictions from large datasets. Unlike rule-based systems such as Symbolic AI, it does not explicitly encode rules. Instead, it uses statistical methods, algorithms, and models to learn from data. The more data it processes, the more accurate and robust its predictions can become, provided the data is relevant and well-curated.

- **Core Principles**

Data-driven AI functions by analyzing historical data to identify trends and relationships that can be generalized. It requires a dataset that is large, diverse, and representative of the real-world scenarios it aims to model. Algorithms such as regression, clustering, and classification are employed to analyze this data. These methods form the foundation of many modern AI systems, including recommendation engines, sentiment analysis tools, and fraud detection systems.

- **Strengths**

One of the main advantages of data-driven AI is its ability to adapt and improve with more data. Unlike systems that require manual updates for new scenarios, data-driven AI can generalize from examples, making it well-suited for dynamic environments like online retail or social media analytics. Furthermore, it excels at tasks like image recognition, natural language processing, and predictive modeling, where patterns in the data are too complex to encode manually.

- **Challenges**

The primary challenge is its reliance on high-quality data. Biases in the data can lead to biased outcomes, which is a significant concern in sensitive applications like hiring or criminal justice. Additionally, the lack of interpretability in many data-driven models (e.g., deep learning) makes them "black boxes," which can hinder their use in applications requiring transparency.

Comparison of Data-Driven AI vs. Machine Learning, as mention in below Table 5.2:

Table 5.2: Data-Driven AI vs. Machine Learning

Aspect	Data-Driven AI	Machine Learning
Definition	AI systems that use data to extract patterns and make decisions without explicit rule encoding.	A subset of data-driven AI focused on learning from data to improve performance over time.
Focus	Broad application of data analysis and decision-making.	Algorithms that learn from data (e.g., supervised, unsupervised, and reinforcement learning).
Core Techniques	Statistical analysis, regression, clustering, association mining.	Neural networks, decision trees, support vector machines, reinforcement learning.
Adaptability	Learns from new data but often requires re-analysis for new patterns.	Continuously improves with more data and feedback.
Applications	Fraud detection, market analysis, recommendation systems.	Self-driving cars, image recognition, conversational AI, and predictive maintenance.
Strengths	Handles large datasets effectively; flexible across various domains.	High accuracy, adaptability, and scalability in dynamic and complex tasks.
Challenges	Requires high-quality data; prone to biases; can lack explainability.	Computationally expensive; black-box nature of complex models; depends heavily on labeled data for training.
Dependency on Data	High dependence on data for analysis but not always iterative learning.	Continuous dependency on data for training, validation, and improvement.
Explainability	Moderate explainability depending on the methods used (e.g., regression models are interpretable).	Often lacks explainability, especially in deep learning models.

Machine Learning (ML)

Machine Learning is a subset of data-driven AI focused on enabling systems to learn from data without explicit programming. It encompasses a wide range of algorithms and techniques that allow machines to improve performance on tasks as they are exposed to more data over time.

▶ Core Principles

ML is typically divided into three main types: supervised learning, unsupervised learning, and reinforcement learning. Supervised learning trains models on labeled datasets, enabling them to predict outcomes for new data. Unsupervised learning, on the other hand, identifies hidden patterns in unlabeled data. Reinforcement learning involves training agents to make decisions by rewarding desired outcomes and penalizing undesirable ones.

- **Strengths**

ML is the backbone of many cutting-edge technologies, such as self-driving cars, personalized medicine, and conversational AI. Its ability to process and learn from massive datasets allows it to tackle problems like image recognition, speech synthesis, and game playing with superhuman accuracy. Additionally, ML's modularity enables it to be integrated into a wide range of industries.

- **Challenges**

Similar to data-driven AI, ML depends heavily on data quality and quantity. Moreover, many ML models, particularly deep learning architectures, lack interpretability. This opaqueness can make it difficult to trust and validate decisions, especially in high-stakes applications like medical diagnosis. Training ML models is also computationally expensive, requiring significant resources for both development and deployment.

Examples of Data-Driven AI and Machine Learning

1. Examples of Data-Driven AI

Fraud Detection in Banking

- Use Case: Identifying fraudulent transactions based on historical data.
- How It Works: A dataset containing records of both fraudulent and legitimate transactions is analyzed to identify patterns, such as unusually large withdrawals or transactions from foreign locations.
- Outcome: The system flags suspicious activities for further review.

2. Recommendation Systems

- Use Case: Suggesting movies, books, or products to users on platforms like Netflix, Amazon, or Spotify.
- How It Works: Uses collaborative filtering or content-based filtering to analyze user preferences and recommend similar items based on historical data.
- Outcome: Personalized recommendations enhance user experience and increase engagement.

3. Market Analysis and Forecasting

- Use Case: Predicting stock prices or market trends based on historical economic data.
- How It Works: Models like time series analysis or regression identify trends, seasonality, and patterns to make future predictions.
- Outcome: Helps businesses and investors make informed decisions.

Examples of Machine Learning

1. Self-Driving Cars (Autonomous Vehicles)

- Use Case: Navigating roads safely without human intervention.
- How It Works: Machine learning models process sensor data, such as images, LiDAR signals, and GPS, to identify objects (e.g., pedestrians, other vehicles), predict their movements, and make real-time decisions.
- Outcome: Enables safe and efficient autonomous driving.

2. Image Recognition

- Use Case: Diagnosing medical conditions from X-rays or identifying objects in photos.
- How It Works: Deep learning algorithms, such as convolutional neural networks (CNNs), learn patterns in images to classify or detect objects.
- Outcome: Systems like Google Lens or AI-assisted medical tools can identify objects, landmarks, or diseases with high accuracy.

3. Chatbots and Virtual Assistants

- Use Case: Providing customer support or personal assistance (e.g., Siri, Alexa, or Google Assistant).
- How It Works: Natural Language Processing (NLP) models learn from large datasets of text to understand and generate human-like responses.
- Outcome: Enhances customer service by providing instant and accurate responses to queries.

Introduction to Machine Learning and Deep Learning based AI

Artificial Intelligence (AI) has evolved significantly over the years, with Machine Learning (ML) and Deep Learning (DL) emerging as dominant paradigms. These approaches are data-driven, enabling systems to learn patterns, make predictions, and automate decision-making without explicit programming. While ML serves as the broader framework, DL is a specialized subset focusing on neural networks with multiple layers. Both methodologies have revolutionized industries, powering technologies like self-driving cars, facial recognition, and personalized medicine.

What is Machine Learning?

Machine Learning is a branch of AI that allows systems to learn from data and improve their performance over time. It involves developing algorithms that can process input data, extract meaningful insights, and generalize these insights to new, unseen scenarios. ML is broadly categorized into three types:

- Supervised Learning: The model is trained on labeled data, where the input-output relationships are explicitly defined. Examples include spam detection in emails and predicting house prices.
- Unsupervised Learning: The model learns patterns and structures from unlabeled data. Clustering and dimensionality reduction are common applications, such as customer segmentation.
- Reinforcement Learning: The model learns through trial and error by interacting with an environment, receiving rewards for desired outcomes. This is commonly used in game-playing AI and robotics.

Machine Learning excels in structured data analysis and is widely used in areas like fraud detection, recommendation systems, and predictive analytics.

What is Deep Learning?

Deep Learning, a subset of ML, uses artificial neural networks inspired by the human brain's structure and functioning. Unlike traditional ML models, DL networks consist of multiple layers (hence the term "deep"), each capable of extracting increasingly complex features from the data. For instance, in an image recognition task, the initial layers might identify edges and shapes, while deeper layers recognize specific objects. DL relies on large datasets and high computational power to train models. Techniques like convolutional neural networks (CNNs) and recurrent neural networks (RNNs) are specialized for tasks such as image processing and sequence prediction, respectively. DL has achieved state-of-the-art results in areas like speech recognition, machine translation, and autonomous driving.

Differences between ML and DL

While ML and DL share a common goal—making predictions and automating tasks—they differ significantly in methodology and application. Traditional ML often relies on manual feature extraction, where domain experts define relevant features. In contrast, DL automates this process, learning features directly from raw data. This makes DL more powerful for unstructured data like images, audio, and text but also more resource-intensive. For instance, a machine learning model for image classification might require preprocessing steps to extract key attributes like color and texture. In contrast, a deep learning model like a CNN learns these attributes as part of its training process. However, this increased capability comes at the cost of higher computational demands and longer training times.

Table 5.3: Differences between Machine Learning (ML) and Deep Learning (DL).

Aspect	Machine Learning (ML)	Deep Learning (DL)
Definition	A subset of AI that enables systems to learn from data and improve over time.	A subset of ML that uses neural networks with multiple layers to process data.
Data Dependency	Performs well with smaller datasets.	Requires large amounts of data for effective training.
Feature Engineering	Requires manual feature extraction and domain expertise to define key features.	Automatically learns features from raw data.
Complexity	Handles structured and simpler problems efficiently.	Excels in handling complex and unstructured data like images and audio.
Computation Needs	Less computationally intensive, suitable for standard systems.	Highly resource-intensive, requiring GPUs or specialized hardware.
Interpretability	Models are generally interpretable, making them easier to explain.	Models often function as "black boxes," making them less interpretable.
Training Time	Faster training time due to simpler algorithms.	Slower training time due to the complexity of deep neural networks.
Applications	Fraud detection, recommendation systems, predictive analytics.	Image recognition, speech processing, autonomous vehicles, NLP.

The above Table 5.3 clearly highlights the distinctions between ML and DL, emphasizing their unique strengths, challenges, and application areas.

Applications of Machine Learning and Deep Learning along with advantages and challenges

Machine Learning (ML) and Deep Learning (DL) have revolutionized industries with their diverse applications. In healthcare, ML is used for predicting patient outcomes and diagnosing diseases by analyzing structured clinical data, while DL excels in analyzing unstructured data, such as medical images like X-rays and MRIs, for disease detection. In finance, ML is vital for fraud detection and credit risk assessment, whereas DL powers personalized solutions like advanced customer service chatbots. E-commerce benefits from ML-driven recommendation engines, offering tailored shopping experiences, while DL is critical for tasks like natural language processing (NLP) in chatbots and machine translation, and autonomous vehicles, where it processes complex sensor and camera data. While ML is easier to implement for structured datasets and small-scale problems, it often requires manual feature engineering and domain expertise. DL, on the other hand, is powerful for handling unstructured and complex data, learning features automatically but requiring massive datasets and significant computational resources. Both face challenges like data bias, which can lead to unfair outcomes, emphasizing the need for ethical use and robust fairness measures as these technologies become more integrated into society. DL particularly shines in areas where unstructured data like images and text dominate, pushing the boundaries of automation and intelligence.

Future of ML and DL

The future of Machine Learning and Deep Learning lies in their convergence with other technologies like edge computing, quantum computing, and neuro-symbolic AI. Researchers are focusing on improving interpretability, reducing computational costs, and creating more generalizable models. As datasets grow larger and computational resources become more accessible, the capabilities of ML and DL will continue to expand, enabling groundbreaking innovations across all sectors. This blend of flexibility, scalability, and adaptability makes ML and DL indispensable tools in solving some of the world's most complex problems, shaping the future of AI-driven solutions.

Applications of symbolic and data driven AI

Applications of Symbolic AI

1. Expert Systems

Expert systems are among the earliest applications of symbolic AI, designed to emulate human decision-making in specialized domains. They rely on a well-defined set of rules and logical reasoning to process inputs and deliver outputs such as diagnoses or recommendations. For instance, MYCIN was developed in the 1970s for medical diagnostics, using predefined rules to suggest treatments for bacterial infections. Similarly, DENDRAL assisted chemists in deducing molecular structures from chemical data. These systems excel in tasks with explicit knowledge that can be encoded in rules, making them highly accurate and reliable in their domains. The ability to explain their reasoning (e.g., showing which rules led to a decision) is another significant advantage. However, expert systems are limited by their scalability; as the complexity of the domain grows, the effort required to encode and maintain the knowledge base increases.

2. Natural Language Understanding (NLU)

Symbolic AI was foundational in the early development of natural language processing, focusing on rule-based approaches to parse and understand text. These systems used predefined grammars and lexicons to analyze sentence structures and extract meaning. For example, early chatbots relied on symbolic methods to match user inputs with scripted responses, providing basic conversational capabilities. While symbolic NLU provided structured and predictable outcomes, its rigidity made it difficult to handle the ambiguities of human language, such as idioms or contextual variations. Modern NLP has largely shifted to machine learning and deep learning approaches for greater flexibility, but symbolic methods are still used in areas requiring precise, rule-based interpretations, such as legal text analysis.

3. Robotics and Task Automation

In robotics, symbolic AI plays a critical role in task planning and automation, especially in controlled environments like manufacturing or logistics. Robots programmed with symbolic planners (e.g., STRIPS) can sequence actions to achieve goals, such as assembling products or navigating warehouses. These systems rely on explicitly defined tasks and constraints, ensuring reliability and predictability. While effective in structured settings, symbolic AI in robotics faces challenges in dynamic environments where unpredictability or incomplete information is common. To address these limitations, hybrid systems combining symbolic reasoning with data-driven learning are being developed, allowing robots to adapt to real-world complexities while maintaining logical planning capabilities.

4. Game Playing

Symbolic AI has been instrumental in developing game-playing systems that excel in strategy and logic-based games like chess. For example, IBM's Deep Blue, a symbolic AI system, famously defeated world champion Garry Kasparov by evaluating millions of potential moves and applying logical strategies encoded in its rules. The success of symbolic AI in this domain stems from its ability to calculate exhaustive possibilities and adhere to strict game rules. However, as games grow more complex, involving dynamic strategies or incomplete information (e.g., poker), symbolic AI's limitations become apparent. In such cases, reinforcement learning and other data-driven methods are more effective.

Applications of Data-Driven AI

1. Healthcare

Data-driven AI has transformed healthcare by enabling predictive analytics, diagnostics, and personalized treatments. Predictive models analyze patient data to identify individuals at risk of chronic diseases, allowing for early interventions. Tools like IBM Watson Health use machine learning to process medical literature, patient histories, and lab results to assist doctors in diagnosis and treatment planning. In addition, deep learning models analyze unstructured data, such as medical images (X-rays, MRIs), to detect diseases like cancer. These systems can achieve diagnostic accuracy comparable to or exceeding that of human experts. Data-driven AI's adaptability and scalability make it a game-changer in healthcare, although it requires large, high-quality datasets and raises concerns about patient data privacy.

2. Finance

In finance, data-driven AI is widely used for fraud detection, credit risk assessment, and algorithmic trading. Fraud detection systems analyze transactional data to identify anomalies, such as unusual spending patterns or suspicious account activity, flagging potential fraud in real-time. Machine learning models also assess creditworthiness by evaluating factors like income, credit history, and spending habits. Algorithmic trading is another significant application, where data-driven AI analyzes market trends and executes trades at high speed based on predictions. These systems improve efficiency and accuracy in decision-making. However, challenges such as biased data and the potential for misuse of AI in financial markets highlight the need for regulatory oversight.

3. E-Commerce

Data-driven AI powers recommendation engines that personalize shopping experiences for customers. Platforms like Amazon and Netflix analyze user behavior, such as browsing history and previous purchases, to suggest products or content tailored to individual preferences. These systems use collaborative filtering, content-based filtering, or hybrid approaches to deliver accurate and dynamic recommendations. In addition to recommendations, data-driven AI supports dynamic pricing strategies by analyzing market demand, competitor pricing, and inventory levels. This enhances profitability while ensuring competitive pricing. The ability to process massive amounts of data in real-time makes AI indispensable in modern e-commerce.

4. Autonomous Vehicles

Autonomous vehicles rely heavily on data-driven AI to process sensor and camera data, enabling real-time navigation and decision-making. Deep learning models identify objects like pedestrians, traffic signs, and vehicles, while machine learning algorithms predict their movements. Companies like Tesla and Waymo use AI to enable self-driving features such as lane detection and collision avoidance. The complex nature of driving environments requires the continuous learning and adaptation capabilities of data-driven AI. These systems are designed to improve over time with exposure to more diverse driving scenarios, making autonomous vehicles safer and more reliable. However, challenges such as ensuring safety in rare edge cases remain significant.

Applications of Symbolic AI

- Expert Systems
- Natural Language Understanding (NLU)
- Robotics and Task Automation
- Game Playing

Applications of Data-Driven AI

- Healthcare
- Finance
- E-Commerce
- Autonomous Vehicles

Figure 5.2: Applications of symbolic and data driven AI.

Symbolic AI and data-driven AI have distinct strengths and applications (Figure 5.2). Symbolic AI thrives in domains requiring explicit reasoning and structured environments, while data-driven AI excels in handling large datasets and dynamic, unstructured scenarios. Together, these approaches offer complementary capabilities, forming the foundation of hybrid AI systems that address a wide range of real-world challenges (Table 5.4).

Table 5.4: Comparison of Applications.

Aspect	Symbolic AI	Data-Driven AI
Healthcare	Rule-based expert systems for diagnostics.	Predictive models for disease detection and treatment personalization.
Finance	Risk assessment using predefined rules.	Fraud detection and algorithmic trading using large datasets.
E-Commerce	Rule-based product recommendations.	Personalized shopping experiences through ML models.
Robotics	Task planning and execution in controlled settings.	Vision-based navigation and object manipulation.
Natural Language	Grammar-based language parsing and translation.	NLP applications like sentiment analysis and chatbots.
Game Playing	Rule-based strategy analysis (e.g., chess).	Adaptive strategies using reinforcement learning.

Interpretable and Explainable AI

Why Interpretable and Explainable AI are Important?

The growing reliance on AI in critical decision-making areas such as healthcare, finance, and criminal justice necessitates understanding how these systems arrive at their conclusions. Users and stakeholders must trust AI systems, and explainability plays a crucial role in building that trust. For instance, a medical diagnosis AI must justify its recommendation to both doctors and patients to ensure confidence in its reliability. Similarly, in the financial sector, an AI system denying a loan must clearly outline the reasoning to comply with transparency regulations. Regulatory frameworks like the EU's General Data Protection Regulation (GDPR) emphasize the "right to explanation," ensuring that decisions affecting individuals are understandable. This is especially important in high-stakes scenarios, such as legal judgments, where opaque systems could perpetuate bias or errors without accountability. Furthermore, ethical AI development benefits from explainability, as it helps uncover potential biases in data or model design, fostering fairness and inclusivity. Explainability is also critical for debugging and improving AI systems. Developers can use insights from explanations to identify flaws in model logic or data representation, optimizing system performance. For organizations, this can reduce risks and improve operational efficiency, ensuring AI systems align with desired outcomes and ethical standards.

Interpretable AI

Interpretable AI models are inherently transparent, allowing humans to directly understand their decision-making processes. These models are typically simpler and more structured, making them suitable for applications requiring high levels of accountability. For example, in healthcare, a linear regression model predicting patient recovery time clearly shows how variables like age, comorbidities, and treatment type contribute to the prediction. This straightforward relationship makes the model's logic easy to understand. Decision trees are another example of interpretable AI. Their branching structure provides a clear path from input to output, showing how specific conditions lead to particular decisions. For instance, in a loan approval system, the tree might outline steps such as "if credit score > 700 and income > $50,000, approve loan." This level of transparency is essential in domains like finance, where regulatory compliance and consumer trust are paramount. However, the simplicity of interpretable models often limits their performance in complex tasks. Problems like image recognition or speech processing, which involve intricate patterns and unstructured data, usually require more complex models that are less interpretable. Thus, while interpretable AI is valuable for transparency, it may not always achieve the accuracy needed for certain advanced applications.

Explainable AI

Explainable AI (XAI) addresses the limitations of complex, opaque models by providing insights into their decision-making processes. Unlike interpretable AI, XAI focuses on generating explanations for black-box models such as deep learning networks. These models are highly accurate in handling complex data, like recognizing objects in images or translating languages, but their intricate architecture makes them difficult to understand without specialized tools. Techniques like LIME (Local Interpretable Model-Agnostic Explanations) and SHAP (SHapley Additive exPlanations) are widely used in XAI. LIME explains individual predictions by creating a simpler, interpretable model that approximates the behavior of the complex model locally (around a specific input). For example, it can highlight which features of a medical image contributed most to a diagnosis. SHAP, on the other hand, assigns importance values to each feature based on its contribution to the prediction, providing a consistent and mathematically grounded explanation. Visualization tools such as saliency maps or Grad-CAM are particularly useful in deep learning. These tools highlight regions of an input image that were most influential in the model's decision. For instance, in diagnosing pneumonia from a chest X-ray, a saliency map might highlight areas of the lungs that the AI deemed significant. While XAI enhances transparency in these scenarios, it may only approximate the true logic of the model, raising questions about its reliability in some cases.

Applications of Interpretable and Explainable AI

▶ **Healthcare**

In healthcare, explainable AI systems provide critical support for diagnostics and treatment planning. For example, an AI model analyzing X-rays to detect cancer must indicate the specific regions or patterns that led to its diagnosis. This ensures doctors can validate the AI's findings and use them confidently in decision-making. Additionally, interpretable AI models, such as those predicting patient risk scores, help clinicians understand how factors like age or pre-existing conditions contribute to outcomes.

▶ **Finance**

Regulatory requirements in finance often demand explainability in AI systems used for credit scoring, fraud detection, or investment recommendations. For instance, if a customer is denied a loan, the AI system must outline the key factors (e.g., credit history, income level) influencing its decision. SHAP values are commonly used in these scenarios to provide feature importance scores, ensuring compliance and building trust with customers.

▶ **Autonomous Vehicles**

AI systems in self-driving cars must make split-second decisions in dynamic environments, such as identifying obstacles or deciding whether to stop at an intersection. Explainable AI helps manufacturers and regulators understand why a vehicle chose a particular action, ensuring safety and reliability. For instance, saliency maps can reveal which aspects of the environment (e.g., pedestrians, traffic signs) influenced the car's behavior.

- **Legal and Criminal Justice**

AI systems used in legal decision-making, such as risk assessments for parole or sentencing, must be transparent to avoid perpetuating biases. Explainability ensures that these systems provide clear, justified reasoning for their recommendations, helping judges and other stakeholders trust and validate the AI's output. For example, if a system categorizes a defendant as high-risk, it should explain the factors leading to that conclusion, such as prior convictions or behavioral patterns.

- **Challenges in Implementing XAI**

Despite its advantages, XAI faces several challenges. One major issue is the trade-off between interpretability and accuracy. Simpler models are easier to understand but may lack the performance needed for complex tasks. In contrast, highly accurate models like deep neural networks are inherently opaque, making them harder to explain. Balancing these priorities is a key challenge in AI development.

Another issue is the subjectivity of explanations. Different stakeholders—developers, regulators, or end-users—may have varying expectations of what constitutes a satisfactory explanation. For example, a technical explanation might satisfy a developer but confuse an end-user. Scalability is also a concern, as generating explanations for large datasets or real-time decisions can be computationally intensive. Moreover, post-hoc explanation techniques like LIME or SHAP may provide approximations that don't fully reflect the model's actual reasoning (Figure 5.3).

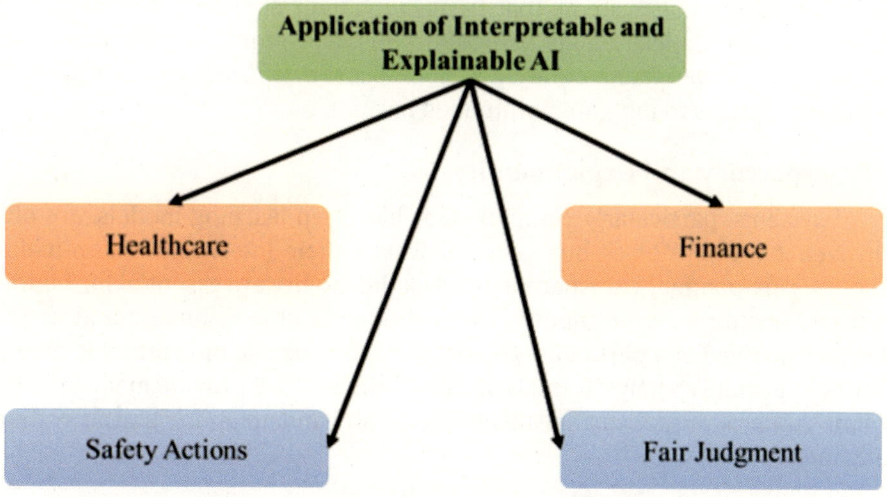

Figure 5.3: Applications of Interpretable and Explainable AI.

Future of Interpretable and Explainable AI

The future of XAI lies in creating hybrid models that combine the interpretability of simpler systems with the accuracy of complex ones. Neuro-symbolic AI, which integrates symbolic reasoning with data-driven learning, is a promising area of research. These systems aim to provide robust performance while maintaining transparency. Additionally, advancements in visualization tools, theoretical frameworks for explainability, and human-centered AI design will further enhance the accessibility and trustworthiness of AI systems. As ethical AI development gains traction, XAI will play a pivotal role in ensuring AI systems are fair, transparent, and aligned with societal values. By making AI systems understandable and accountable, XAI will foster greater adoption across industries and support the responsible deployment of advanced technologies.

Ethics of AI

The ethics of AI addresses the moral principles, societal impacts, and challenges associated with developing and deploying artificial intelligence technologies. As AI systems increasingly influence critical areas such as healthcare, finance, governance, and law enforcement, ethical considerations ensure that these technologies are designed and used responsibly, respecting human rights and values.

Core Ethical Principles in AI

1. Fairness and Bias Mitigation

AI systems often reflect biases present in their training data, leading to unfair or discriminatory outcomes. For instance, an AI model trained on biased hiring data might favor one gender over another. The ethical imperative is to ensure fairness by designing systems that treat individuals equitably. Techniques like diverse training datasets, bias detection tools, and regular audits can reduce biases and improve system equity. Developers and organizations must prioritize inclusive practices to mitigate unintended harm.

2. Transparency and Explainability

AI systems, particularly complex ones like deep learning models, are often criticized for their "black-box" nature, where their internal decision-making processes are opaque. Transparency and explainability are essential for building trust and enabling accountability. Users should be able to understand how an AI system arrived at a particular decision. Techniques like interpretable models, feature importance analysis, and tools like LIME or SHAP provide mechanisms to explain AI decisions, ensuring stakeholders can validate and trust the system's outcomes.

3. Privacy and Data Protection

AI relies heavily on large datasets, often containing sensitive personal information, raising concerns about privacy and misuse. Ethical AI development emphasizes robust data protection practices, such as anonymization, encryption, and collecting only necessary data. Regulations like GDPR mandate transparency in data usage and obtaining user consent. Ensuring privacy not only aligns with ethical standards but also fosters user confidence and compliance with legal frameworks.

4. Accountability and Responsibility

AI systems can cause harm or errors, such as incorrect medical diagnoses or biased loan approvals, raising questions about accountability. Developers, organizations, and policymakers must clearly define who is responsible for AI-driven actions. Ethical AI frameworks encourage assigning accountability to developers and organizations, along with implementing fail-safe mechanisms to prevent harm. Transparent documentation and monitoring systems are essential to address failures and uphold ethical standards.

5. Safety and Security

Ensuring that AI systems operate safely and reliably is critical, particularly in high-risk applications like autonomous vehicles or healthcare. Adversarial attacks and system vulnerabilities pose significant risks. Ethical AI practices involve rigorous testing under real-world conditions, implementing cybersecurity measures, and designing systems resilient to exploitation. For sensitive domains like military AI, international cooperation is needed to establish ethical usage guidelines and prevent misuse.

Societal and Global Impacts

1. Job Displacement and Economic Inequality

AI-driven automation is transforming industries, automating repetitive tasks, and creating efficiency. However, it also threatens job security for workers in affected sectors, exacerbating economic inequality. Ethical AI development should prioritize strategies to mitigate these effects, such as investing in workforce upskilling, reskilling, and creating new opportunities in AI-related fields. Policymakers and organizations must ensure that AI's economic benefits are distributed equitably across society.

2. Human Rights and Autonomy

AI systems often impact fundamental human rights, including autonomy and dignity. For example, automated systems in law enforcement or social services can affect individuals' lives without adequate oversight. Ethical AI should prioritize respecting human rights by ensuring transparency, fairness, and human involvement in decision-making processes. Governments and organizations must establish safeguards to prevent AI systems from undermining individual freedoms.

3. Environmental Sustainability

The training and operation of large AI models consume significant computational resources, contributing to environmental challenges. For example, the energy requirements of training large deep learning models can result in substantial carbon emissions. Ethical AI practices encourage the development of energy-efficient algorithms and the use of renewable energy sources to minimize environmental impacts. Researchers and organizations must balance AI advancements with sustainability goals.

4. Weaponization and Misuse

The use of AI in weapon systems and mass surveillance poses serious ethical concerns. Autonomous weapons could operate without human intervention, raising questions about accountability and potential harm. Similarly, AI-driven surveillance systems may infringe on privacy and human rights. Global collaboration is essential to create policies and treaties regulating AI in these domains, ensuring its use aligns with humanitarian principles and does not threaten global stability.

Frameworks and Guidelines

Ethical AI principles have been formalized in several frameworks. The Asilomar AI Principles advocate for shared benefits, accountability, and transparency in AI development. The EU Ethical Guidelines for Trustworthy AI emphasize fairness, privacy, and human oversight, aligning AI systems with societal values. Similarly, UNESCO's AI Ethics Recommendations call for global cooperation to ensure ethical practices across borders. These frameworks provide actionable blueprints to guide ethical AI development and deployment.

Challenges in Implementing Ethical AI

- **Ambiguity in Ethical Standards**

Ethical norms and priorities vary across cultures, regions, and industries, complicating the establishment of universal standards. Developers and policymakers must navigate these differences to create flexible yet robust ethical frameworks.

- **Balancing Innovation and Regulation**

Striking a balance between fostering innovation and enforcing regulations is challenging. Over-regulation may stifle progress, while under-regulation could lead to unethical practices. Policymakers and organizations must create adaptive frameworks that allow innovation while safeguarding societal values.

▶ **Complexity of AI Systems**

The increasing complexity of AI systems makes it difficult to ensure transparency, fairness, and accountability. Developers must invest in tools and methodologies that simplify the understanding and monitoring of these systems without compromising performance.

▶ **Resource Constraints**

Developing ethical AI requires significant investments in time, expertise, and infrastructure. Smaller organizations may lack the resources to implement comprehensive ethical practices, highlighting the need for accessible tools and shared resources to democratize ethical AI development.

Benefits and Risks of AI

Artificial Intelligence (AI) has revolutionized industries by automating processes, enhancing decision-making, and enabling innovations. However, alongside its benefits, AI poses significant risks that require careful consideration and management. Understanding both aspects is crucial for harnessing AI's potential responsibly.

Benefits of AI

Enhanced Efficiency and Productivity: AI excels in automating repetitive and time-consuming tasks, allowing organizations to optimize operations and reduce human error. For example, AI-driven automation in manufacturing ensures consistent quality and faster production. In business, AI-powered tools like chatbots provide 24/7 customer support, improving service delivery.

Improved Decision-Making: AI analyzes vast datasets quickly and provides insights that support evidence-based decisions. In healthcare, AI algorithms assist in diagnosing diseases by analyzing medical images, while in finance, predictive analytics identify market trends and detect fraud. These capabilities enhance accuracy and reduce reliance on intuition alone.

Innovation and Problem-Solving: AI enables innovations in fields such as robotics, autonomous vehicles, and natural language processing. Self-driving cars use AI to navigate safely, and AI-driven language models improve communication through real-time translations and content generation. Such breakthroughs solve complex problems and open new opportunities for growth.

Personalization: AI tailors services and products to individual preferences, enhancing user experiences. Platforms like Amazon and Netflix use AI to recommend products and content based on user behavior. This personalization drives customer satisfaction and loyalty.

Risks of AI

- **Bias and Discrimination**

AI systems can inherit biases from their training data, leading to discriminatory outcomes. For instance, biased hiring algorithms may favor specific demographics, perpetuating inequality. Addressing this risk requires diverse datasets and regular audits to ensure fairness.

- **Privacy Concerns**

AI relies heavily on data, raising concerns about privacy and data misuse. For example, facial recognition technology can infringe on individual privacy if used for mass surveillance without consent. Ethical AI practices must prioritize data protection and transparency.

- **Job Displacement**

Automation powered by AI threatens to replace jobs, particularly in sectors like manufacturing and retail. While AI creates new roles in technology and data analysis, the transition requires significant workforce reskilling and upskilling to mitigate unemployment.

- **Lack of Transparency**

Complex AI models, such as deep learning systems, often operate as "black boxes," making it difficult to understand their decision-making processes. This lack of transparency can erode trust, particularly in sensitive applications like healthcare and criminal justice.

- **Security Risks**

AI systems are vulnerable to cyberattacks and adversarial exploitation. Hackers can manipulate AI models to produce incorrect outputs or gain unauthorized access to sensitive systems. Robust security measures are necessary to safeguard AI applications.

- **Balancing Benefits and Risks**

While AI offers transformative benefits, its risks must be managed to ensure responsible adoption. Governments, organizations, and researchers must collaborate to establish ethical guidelines, promote transparency, and invest in public awareness. Encouraging innovation while addressing challenges will pave the way for sustainable AI development.

Table 5.5: Benefits vs. Risks of AI

Aspect	Benefits	Risks
Efficiency	Automates repetitive tasks, reduces errors, and increases productivity.	Job displacement due to automation in various industries.
Decision-Making	Provides data-driven insights for accurate and timely decisions.	Lack of transparency in complex models can erode trust.

Aspect	Benefits	Risks
Innovation	Enables breakthroughs in autonomous vehicles, robotics, and language processing.	Security vulnerabilities can lead to adversarial attacks and data breaches.
Personalization	Tailors products and services to individual preferences, improving user experiences.	Bias in algorithms can lead to discriminatory outcomes.
Data Utilization	Analyzes large datasets to uncover valuable insights.	Raises privacy concerns due to reliance on personal and sensitive data.

The dual nature of AI's benefits and risks highlights the need for a balanced approach to its development and implementation (Table 5.5). By leveraging its strengths while addressing ethical, security, and societal challenges, AI can drive progress and improve lives responsibly. Proactive measures, such as robust regulations, ethical guidelines, and continuous education, are essential to ensure AI serves humanity effectively.

Conclusion

This chapter provides an overview of AI's evolution from Symbolic AI to Data-driven approaches like Machine Learning, highlighting their applications and challenges. It emphasizes the importance of Explainable AI for transparency and discusses ethical considerations, benefits, and risks, offering insights into AI's transformative potential and the need for responsible development. Next chapter introduces the concept of learning in AI, emphasizing its importance and various types: supervised, unsupervised, semi-supervised, and reinforcement learning. It covers foundational algorithms for each learning type, the basics of reinforcement learning including agents and environments, and methods for evaluating and optimizing learning models such as cross-validation, hyperparameter tuning, and addressing overfitting and underfitting.

Exercise

- Define Symbolic AI and explain its primary applications. How does it differ from Data-driven AI?
- What are the main types of Machine Learning, and how do they differ in their approach to learning from data? Provide examples for each.
- Describe two real-world applications for Symbolic AI and two for Data-driven AI. What makes each approach suitable for its respective application?
- What is Interpretable and Explainable AI (XAI)? Why is it crucial in high-stakes industries such as healthcare and finance?

- Discuss the ethical challenges of AI. How can issues like bias, lack of transparency, and accountability be addressed effectively?
- List and explain three benefits and three risks of AI. How can organizations mitigate these risks while leveraging AI's potential?
- Compare and contrast the roles of Symbolic AI and Machine Learning in autonomous systems like self-driving cars.
- How does Explainable AI enhance trust and accountability in AI systems? Provide examples of tools or techniques used for explainability.
- What are the environmental implications of training large AI models? Suggest measures to reduce the carbon footprint of AI technologies.
- In your opinion, what role should governments play in regulating AI development and deployment? Provide examples of existing frameworks or guidelines.

6

Learning and Adaptation in AI

Introduction

Learning in AI involves developing systems that can adapt, make predictions, and improve over time using data and feedback. It is a cornerstone of modern AI, enabling machines to solve complex problems, recognize patterns, and make intelligent decisions without explicit programming.

Objective

The objective of this chapter is to provide a foundational understanding of the types and methods of learning in AI, including supervised, unsupervised, and reinforcement learning. By the end, readers will be equipped with knowledge of key algorithms, their applications, and techniques to optimize and evaluate AI models for effective problem-solving.

Introduction to Learning in AI

Learning in Artificial Intelligence (AI) is the process by which systems acquire knowledge, recognize patterns, and adapt their behavior based on data and experiences. Unlike traditional programming, where explicit instructions are provided for every task, learning systems infer rules and relationships from examples. This capability allows AI to tackle complex, dynamic, and data-rich problems that would be infeasible to solve with predefined algorithms alone. The concept of learning in AI is inspired by human cognition and the way humans improve through observation, practice, and feedback. Machines achieve this through various learning paradigms, such as supervised learning, where they learn from labeled examples, or reinforcement learning, where they adapt by interacting with an environment and receiving feedback in the form of rewards or penalties. These paradigms empower AI systems to generalize from past data and make predictions or decisions in novel situations.

Learning in AI is foundational to many real-world applications, including image recognition, natural language processing, autonomous driving, and recommendation systems. For instance, a recommendation engine learns user preferences from historical data to suggest products or services tailored to individual tastes. Similarly, self-driving cars learn to navigate roads by analyzing vast amounts of sensor data and scenarios. A critical aspect of AI learning is its iterative nature. As new data becomes available, models are retrained or updated to reflect current trends or environments. This adaptability ensures that AI systems remain effective over time, even as circumstances change. For example, fraud detection systems continuously learn from new patterns of fraudulent activity to stay ahead of evolving threats. Learning in AI represents a shift from rigid, rule-based systems to adaptive, data-driven approaches capable of solving a diverse range of problems. It enables machines to mimic intelligent behavior, making them more versatile and effective across various domains. This capability underpins the transformative impact of AI on industries and everyday life, driving advancements in technology and innovation.

Definition and Importance of Learning in AI

Learning in Artificial Intelligence (AI) refers to the ability of machines to gain knowledge, identify patterns, and make decisions based on data and experiences, rather than relying solely on explicit programming. This process involves creating models that can generalize from observed data and adapt to new inputs, enabling AI systems to function intelligently and autonomously in dynamic environments.

Importance

The importance of learning in AI lies in its ability to enable machines to handle complex, data-driven tasks that would be challenging or impossible to program manually. By learning from data, AI systems can adapt to new situations, improve over time, and provide accurate results in diverse scenarios. This capability is critical in addressing real-world challenges, such as predicting market trends, diagnosing diseases, and recognizing speech or images.

Advantage of learning in AI is its capacity for generalization

Once a machine learning model is trained on a dataset, it can apply the knowledge to unseen data, allowing it to solve problems without direct supervision. For instance, an AI trained to recognize cats in images can identify new images of cats it has never seen before. This adaptability makes AI versatile across a wide range of applications.

Another aspect of its importance is scalability

Traditional programming requires extensive manual effort to define rules for every scenario, which becomes impractical as the complexity of the problem increases. Learning-based AI systems, however, scale effectively with data. The more data they are exposed to, the better they perform. This makes them indispensable in data-intensive fields such as healthcare, finance, and e-commerce. Continuous improvement is another critical benefit of AI learning.

Models can be updated as new data becomes available, ensuring they remain relevant and effective. For example, spam detection algorithms in email systems are continuously refined to recognize evolving patterns of unwanted messages, improving user experience and security.

Learning also contributes to the automation of decision-making. By analyzing large datasets, AI can uncover patterns and insights that might not be immediately apparent to humans. This ability enables faster, more accurate decisions in fields like autonomous vehicles, fraud detection, and medical diagnostics. Learning is fundamental to the development and success of AI. It allows machines to go beyond rigid programming, adapt to real-world challenges, and deliver intelligent solutions. By enabling generalization, scalability, continuous improvement, and automated decision-making, learning in AI drives advancements across industries and enhances the potential of technology in solving global problems.

Table 6.1: Benefits of Learning in AI

Aspect	Description
Generalization	Models apply knowledge from training data to new, unseen situations.
Scalability	AI systems can handle large, complex datasets effectively.
Continuous Improvement	Models adapt and improve over time with new data.
Automation	Enables machines to make fast, accurate, and consistent decisions.
Versatility	Applicable across diverse domains, from healthcare to finance and beyond.
Insight Discovery	AI identifies patterns and relationships in data that are not obvious to humans.

The above Table 6.1 summarizes the key benefits of learning in AI, highlighting its role in driving intelligent, adaptive, and efficient solutions.

Types of learning: Supervised, Unsupervised, Semi-supervised, and Reinforcement Learning

Types of Learning in AI

Learning in AI can be categorized into four main types: supervised learning, unsupervised learning, semi-supervised learning, and reinforcement learning. Each type serves different purposes based on the nature of the data and the desired outcomes.

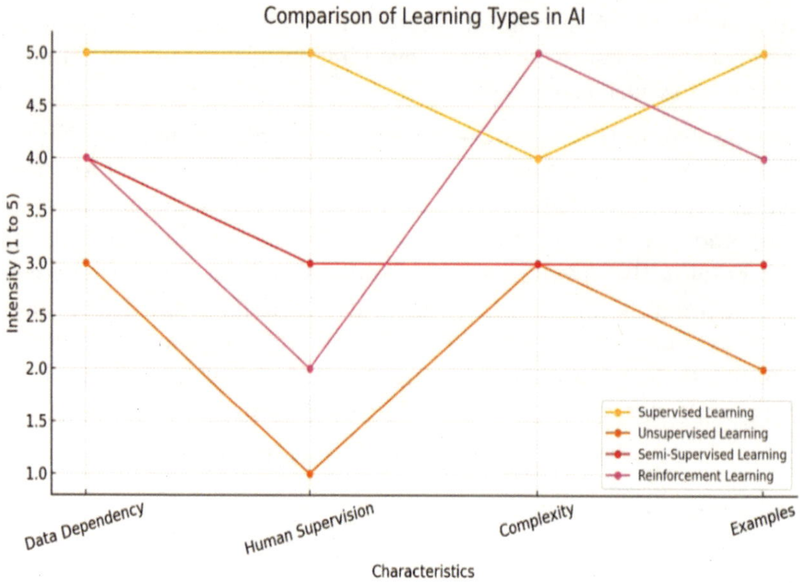

Figure 6.1: compares different types of learning in AI.

The Figure 6.1 compares different types of learning in AI—supervised, un-supervised, semi-supervised, and re-inforcement learning—across characteristics like data dependency, human supervision, complexity, and examples. Supervised learning scores highest in human supervision and examples, while re-inforcement learning excels in complexity. Unsupervised learning has lower human supervision requirements, making it ideal for exploratory analysis.

1. Supervised Learning

In supervised learning, the model is trained on labeled data, where each input is associated with a known output. The goal is to learn a mapping from inputs to outputs so that the model can predict the output for unseen data. Common tasks in supervised learning include classification (e.g., identifying spam emails) and regression (e.g., predicting house prices).

- Examples: Linear Regression, Decision Trees, Support Vector Machines (SVM), Neural Networks.
- Advantages: Highly accurate for well-labeled datasets and straightforward to interpret.
- Challenges: Requires large, labeled datasets, which can be costly and time-consuming to obtain.

2. Unsupervised Learning

Unsupervised learning works with unlabeled data. The model seeks to discover patterns or structures within the data without any explicit guidance. It is commonly used for clustering (grouping similar items) and dimensionality reduction (simplifying data representation).

- Examples: K-Means Clustering, Principal Component Analysis (PCA), Hierarchical Clustering.
- Advantages: Does not require labeled data, making it useful for exploratory data analysis.
- Challenges: Results can be harder to interpret, and it requires domain expertise to validate the discovered patterns.

3. Semi-Supervised Learning

Semi-supervised learning combines aspects of supervised and unsupervised learning. It uses a small amount of labeled data alongside a larger pool of unlabeled data. The labeled data guides the learning process, while the unlabeled data helps the model generalize better.

- Examples: Techniques that combine supervised algorithms with unsupervised methods like clustering or self-training.
- Advantages: Reduces the need for extensive labeled data while improving model performance.
- Challenges: Balancing the influence of labeled and unlabeled data can be complex.

4. Reinforcement Learning

Reinforcement learning involves training an agent to interact with an environment and learn optimal actions by maximizing cumulative rewards. It differs from other types of learning by focusing on sequential decision-making and learning from feedback.

- Key Concepts: Agents, environments, rewards, actions, and states.
- Examples: Q-Learning, Policy Gradients.
- Advantages: Effective for tasks requiring long-term planning, such as robotics and game AI.
- Challenges: Computationally expensive, requires careful design of reward structures, and can be unstable.

Common Algorithms: Linear Regression, Decision Trees, Support Vector Machines (SVM), Neural Networks

Common Algorithms in AI Learning

1. Linear Regression

Linear Regression is a fundamental algorithm used for regression tasks, where the goal is to predict a continuous output variable based on one or more input variables. It assumes a linear relationship between the independent variables (features) and the dependent variable (target). The model fits a line, represented by the equation $y=mx+c$, where m is the slope, c is the intercept, and y is the predicted output.Linear regression minimizes the sum of squared differences between observed and predicted values to find the best-fitting line. It is intuitive and easy to interpret, making it an excellent starting point for regression problems. However, it assumes that the relationship between variables is linear, which can be a limitation for more complex datasets.

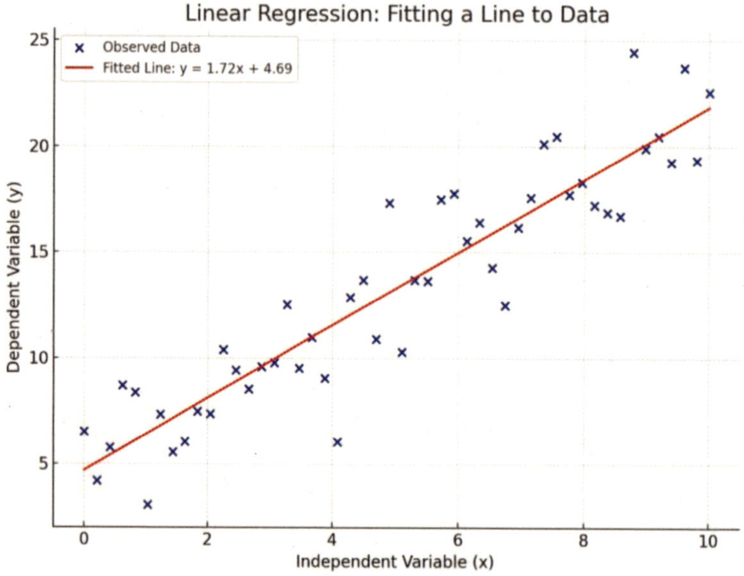

Figure 6.2: linear Regression

The Figure 6.2 illustrates a linear regression model fitting a line to a set of observed data points. The red line represents the best-fitting linear equation ($y=mx+c$) obtained by minimizing the sum of squared differences between the actual data points (blue dots) and the predicted values on the line. This visualization demonstrates the simplicity and interpretability of linear regression in capturing linear relationships in data.

This algorithm is widely used in applications such as forecasting sales, predicting house prices, and analyzing relationships in scientific studies. Despite its simplicity, linear regression can be sensitive to outliers, multicollinearity among features, and non-linear patterns in data.

2. Decision Trees

Decision Trees are non-parametric models used for both classification and regression tasks. They work by dividing data into subsets based on the values of input features, creating a tree-like structure. Each internal node represents a decision rule on a feature, each branch represents an outcome of the rule, and each leaf node represents a predicted output. Decision trees are easy to visualize and interpret, making them valuable for understanding decision-making processes. They can handle both numerical and categorical data and are robust to outliers. However, decision trees are prone to overfitting, especially when they grow too deep, capturing noise in the data rather than meaningful patterns. Applications of decision trees include fraud detection, risk assessment, and medical diagnosis. To mitigate overfitting, techniques such as pruning, setting a maximum tree depth, or using ensemble methods like Random Forests can be employed.

3. Support Vector Machines (SVM)

Support Vector Machines (SVM) are powerful supervised learning algorithms primarily used for classification tasks. SVM works by finding the hyperplane that best separates data points of different classes in a multi-dimensional space. For non-linear data, SVM uses kernel functions to transform input features into higher-dimensional spaces where a linear hyperplane can be found. SVM excels in high-dimensional spaces and is effective for datasets with a clear margin of separation between classes. It also works well for small datasets, as it focuses on support vectors (critical data points) rather than all data points. However, SVM can be computationally intensive for large datasets and is sensitive to the choice of kernel functions and hyperparameters. Applications of SVM include text classification, image recognition, and bioinformatics. It is a robust algorithm for complex problems but requires careful tuning to achieve optimal performance.

4. Neural Networks

Neural Networks are inspired by the human brain and consist of interconnected layers of nodes (neurons). Each neuron processes inputs through a weighted sum and applies an activation function to introduce non-linearity. Neural networks can model complex relationships and patterns in data, making them suitable for a wide range of tasks. Neural networks are particularly powerful for large datasets and applications like image recognition, natural language processing, and autonomous systems. However, they are computationally expensive, require significant amounts of labeled data, and can overfit without proper regularization techniques like dropout or early stopping. Despite these challenges, neural networks form the foundation of deep learning, which uses multi-layer architectures to solve highly complex problems. Their flexibility and adaptability make them indispensable in modern AI.

Table 6.2: Comparison of Common Algorithms

Algorithm	Type	Strengths	Limitations	Applications
Linear Regression	Regression	Simple, interpretable, fast for small datasets	Assumes linear relationships, sensitive to outliers	House price prediction, trend analysis
Decision Trees	Classification/ Regression	Easy to interpret, handles categorical and numerical data, robust to outliers	Prone to overfitting, less effective for high-dimensional data	Fraud detection, medical diagnosis
SVM	Classification	Effective in high-dimensional spaces, robust for complex problems	Computationally expensive, sensitive to kernel and hyperparameter selection	Text classification, image recognition
Neural Networks	Classification/ Regression	Powerful for complex and large datasets, models non-linear relationships	Requires large datasets, computationally intensive, risk of overfitting	Image recognition, NLP, autonomous systems

This Table 6.2 reviews the key characteristics of each algorithm, highlighting their strengths, limitations, and applications for a comprehensive understanding

Common Algorithms: K-Means Clustering, Principal Component Analysis (PCA), Hierarchical Clustering

1. K-Means Clustering

K-Means Clustering is a popular unsupervised learning algorithm used for partitioning a dataset into k distinct clusters. The algorithm works iteratively to minimize the sum of squared distances between data points and the centroids of their respective clusters. It initializes k centroids, assigns each data point to the nearest centroid, and updates the centroids based on the average of points within each cluster. K-Means is highly efficient for large datasets and straightforward to implement. However, the performance depends on the selection of k, which is typically chosen using methods like the elbow method. The algorithm assumes that clusters are spherical and evenly distributed, which might not hold in all datasets.

- Applications: Customer segmentation, image compression, and pattern recognition.
- Strengths: Simple, scalable, and computationally efficient.
- Limitations: Sensitive to outliers, initialization, and non-globular clusters.

2. Principal Component Analysis (PCA)

PCA is a dimensionality reduction technique used to transform high-dimensional data into a lower-dimensional space while retaining as much variance as possible. It identifies principal components, which are orthogonal axes that capture the maximum variance in the data. By projecting the data onto these components, PCA simplifies data representation while reducing redundancy. PCA is widely used for visualization, noise reduction, and preprocessing in machine learning pipelines. It helps in understanding the structure of high-dimensional data and removing irrelevant features, making models faster and more efficient.

- Applications: Image compression, financial modeling, and bioinformatics.
- Strengths: Effective for high-dimensional data and improves model efficiency.
- Limitations: Sensitive to scaling, assumes linear relationships, and may lose interpretability of original features.

3. Hierarchical Clustering

Hierarchical Clustering is an unsupervised algorithm that builds a hierarchy of clusters. It operates either in an agglomerative manner (bottom-up) by merging the closest clusters or in a divisive manner (top-down) by splitting clusters recursively. The results are often visualized using a dendrogram, which shows the merging or splitting process. Unlike K-Means, hierarchical clustering does not require the number of clusters to be specified in advance. It is well-suited for smaller datasets and provides a detailed clustering structure. However, it is computationally expensive and may struggle with large datasets.

- Applications: Gene expression analysis, document clustering, and social network analysis.
- Strengths: Does not require predefining k, produces a detailed clustering hierarchy.
- Limitations: Computationally intensive, sensitive to noise and outliers.

Basic concepts: Agents, Environments, Rewards

1. Agents

In reinforcement learning, an agent is the decision-making entity that interacts with the environment to achieve a specific goal. The agent observes the environment, takes actions, and learns from the consequences of these actions to maximize cumulative rewards. The agent's primary responsibility is to develop a policy—a mapping from states (or observations) to actions—that guides its decisions. Agents can vary in complexity depending on the task. A simple agent might use predefined rules to make decisions, while a sophisticated agent may employ advanced machine learning algorithms, such as deep reinforcement learning, to adapt and optimize its behavior dynamically. The learning process involves trial and error, where the agent explores various actions and evaluates their outcomes to refine its policy over time. The design of an agent includes components like sensors (to perceive the environment) and actuators (to perform actions). For example, in autonomous driving, the agent uses sensors like cameras and LIDAR to perceive its surroundings and actuators like steering wheels and brakes to control the vehicle. An effective agent is one that balances exploration (trying new actions to discover better strategies) and exploitation (leveraging known actions to maximize rewards).

2. Environments

The environment is the external system with which the agent interacts. It provides the context for the agent's actions and defines the rules of the task. The environment receives actions from the agent, transitions to a new state based on those actions, and provides feedback (rewards) to the agent. This interaction forms a feedback loop, enabling the agent to learn and adapt. Environments can be deterministic or stochastic. In deterministic environments, the outcome of an action is predictable, while in stochastic environments, there is inherent uncertainty in the results of actions. For instance, a chessboard is a deterministic environment because the rules and outcomes of moves are fixed. In contrast, a self-driving car operates in a stochastic environment, where factors like traffic, weather, and pedestrian behavior introduce uncertainty. The complexity of the environment significantly impacts the design and performance of the agent. Simple environments allow agents to learn optimal policies relatively quickly, while complex environments with high dimensionality or dynamic rules require more sophisticated approaches, such as function approximation and deep reinforcement learning.

3. Rewards

A reward is the feedback signal that the environment provides to the agent after it takes an action. Rewards guide the agent's learning process by indicating the desirability of its actions. The agent's objective is to maximize the cumulative reward over time, which often involves balancing short-term and long-term gains. Rewards can be immediate or delayed. Immediate rewards are provided right after an action, while delayed rewards require the agent to evaluate sequences of actions to achieve a goal. For example, in a maze-solving task, the agent might receive a small reward for each correct step and a large reward upon reaching the exit. Delayed rewards make the learning process more challenging, as the agent must associate actions with their long-term outcomes. The reward function is crucial in reinforcement learning because it defines the task for the agent. A poorly designed reward function can lead to suboptimal or unintended behavior.

For instance, if a robot is rewarded solely for moving, it might move in circles without completing its task. Therefore, careful consideration is needed to design reward functions that align with the desired goals.

Markov Decision Processes (MDPs)

Markov Decision Processes (MDPs) provide a mathematical framework for modeling decision-making problems where outcomes are partly random and partly under the control of a decision-maker. An MDP is defined by four key components:

- States (S): The possible situations or configurations the system can be in.
- Actions (A): The set of choices available to the agent in each state.
- Transition Probabilities (P): The probability of transitioning to a new state given the current state and action.
- Rewards (R): The feedback signal that indicates the value of being in a particular state or taking a specific action.

Working of MDPs

At each step, the agent observes the current state, chooses an action, and moves to a new state based on the transition probabilities. It receives a reward associated with the action taken. The goal of the agent is to find an optimal policy—a strategy that specifies the best action to take in each state to maximize the cumulative reward over time. MDPs assume the Markov Property, which states that the future state depends only on the current state and action, not on the sequence of previous states. This property simplifies the decision-making process and makes MDPs suitable for various applications.

Applications of MDPs

MDPs are used in diverse fields such as robotics, game AI, and finance. For instance, in robotics, MDPs can model navigation tasks where the robot must choose the best path to reach a target while avoiding obstacles. In finance, MDPs are used to optimize investment strategies by modeling market dynamics and decision outcomes. The Figure 6.3 illustrates a simple MDP with four states and various actions connecting them. Each edge is labeled with an action and its associated reward. This graph demonstrates how states are interconnected, and the agent's goal is to navigate through these states to maximize cumulative rewards.

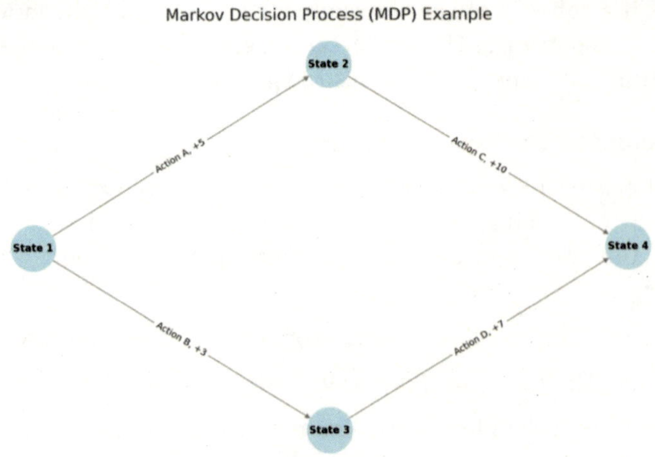

Figure 6.3: simple MDP Four States.

MDPs are a cornerstone of reinforcement learning, forming the basis for algorithms like Q-learning and policy gradients, which are used to solve complex sequential decision-making problems.

Q-learning and Policy Gradients

Q-Learning

Q-Learning is a model-free reinforcement learning algorithm that focuses on learning the value of actions in specific states, known as Q-values. The algorithm uses a Q-table, where each entry corresponds to a state-action pair. By iteratively updating the Q-values based on rewards received and expected future rewards, Q-Learning enables the agent to learn an optimal policy. The core equation is:

$$Q(s,a) \leftarrow Q(s,a) + \alpha[r + \gamma \max_{a} Q(s',a) - Q(s,a)]$$

- **States (s)**: Current state of the agent.
- **Actions (a)**: Choices available in the state.
- **Reward (r)**: Feedback received after taking an action.
- **Learning rate (α)**: Determines how much new information overrides old information.
- **Discount factor (γ)**: Balances immediate rewards against future rewards.

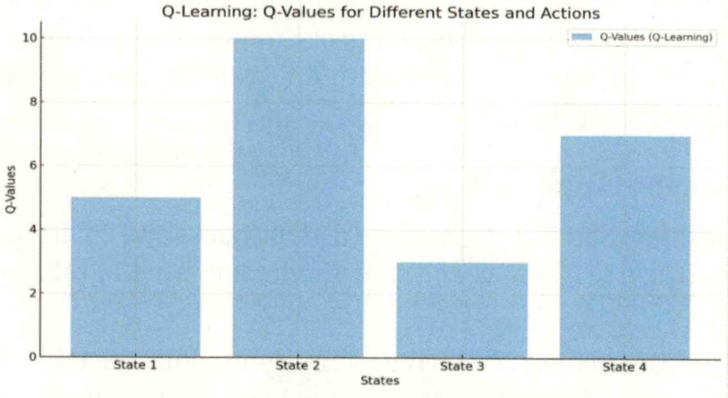

Figure 6.4: Q-values for Different States.

The bar chart above represents Q-values for different states and actions (Figure 6.4). These values guide the agent to select actions with the highest

Policy Gradients

Policy gradients are a class of algorithms in reinforcement learning that optimize a policy directly rather than relying on value functions. The policy maps states to probabilities of taking each action. Policy gradients use gradient ascent to maximize the cumulative expected reward:

$$\nabla J(\theta) = \mathbb{E}\left[\nabla \log \pi_\theta(a|s) \cdot G_t\right]$$

Policy ($\pi_\theta(a|s)$): The probability of taking action aaa in state s, parameterized by θ.

Gradient ($\nabla J(\theta)$): Adjusts policy parameters to improve expected rewards.

Return (Gt): Total discounted reward from time t.

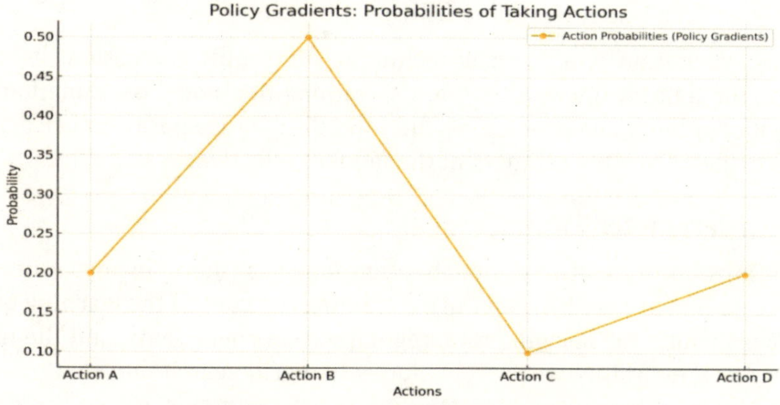

Figure 6.5: Policy Gradients

The line chart above visualizes action probabilities obtained from policy gradients. Unlike Q-Learning, which selects the best action deterministically, policy gradients sample actions based on learned probabilities, enabling stochastic exploration (Figure 6.5).

Comparison and Applications

- Q-Learning: Suitable for discrete action spaces and environments where value-based learning is effective. Commonly used in robotics and game AI.
- Policy Gradients: Preferred for continuous action spaces and environments requiring stochastic policies, such as autonomous driving or complex robotics.

Both approaches are fundamental in reinforcement learning, offering unique strengths for solving a variety of sequential decision-making problems

Evaluation and Optimization of Learning Models

Evaluation and optimization are critical steps in the development and deployment of machine learning models. They ensure that models perform well on unseen data, remain robust across various scenarios, and achieve the desired objectives efficiently.

1. Model Evaluation

Evaluation involves assessing the performance of a model on a dataset that was not used during training. This step helps determine how well the model generalizes to new data. Common evaluation metrics depend on the type of task:

- For regression: Metrics like Mean Squared Error (MSE), Mean Absolute Error (MAE), and $R2$ score are used.
- For classification: Metrics include accuracy, precision, recall, F1-score, and Area Under the Curve (AUC).

Cross-validation is a popular technique for robust evaluation. It involves splitting the dataset into multiple folds, training the model on some folds, and testing it on others. The process repeats, and the average performance across all folds provides a reliable estimate of the model's effectiveness.

2. Hyperparameter Tuning

Optimization of learning models often involves tuning hyperparameters—parameters that are not learned during training but control the learning process. Examples include the learning rate, regularization coefficients, and the number of layers in a neural network. Techniques like grid search and random search systematically explore combinations of hyperparameter values to find the best configuration. More advanced approaches, such as Bayesian optimization and automated machine learning (AutoML), leverage probabilistic models or heuristics to efficiently navigate the hyperparameter space.

3. Addressing Overfitting and Underfitting

Two common challenges in machine learning are overfitting and underfitting. Overfitting occurs when the model learns noise and details in the training data, performing poorly on unseen data. Underfitting happens when the model is too simple to capture the underlying patterns in the data.

Techniques to address overfitting include:

- Regularization: Adding constraints like L1 (Lasso) or L2 (Ridge) regularization to the optimization process.
- Dropout: Randomly dropping neurons in neural networks during training.
- Pruning: Reducing the complexity of decision trees.

To combat underfitting, more complex models, additional features, or extended training time can be used.

4. Monitoring and Optimization

Optimization involves improving the model's performance iteratively. Key strategies include:

- Learning Rate Schedules: Adjusting the learning rate dynamically during training.
- Data Augmentation: Increasing dataset diversity using transformations like rotations or flips for images.
- Early Stopping: Halting training when the validation performance stops improving, preventing overfitting.

Additionally, monitoring metrics during training, such as loss and validation error, provides insights into the model's learning dynamics, helping identify potential issues early.

Cross-validation

Cross-validation is a robust evaluation technique used to assess the generalization performance of a machine learning model. It divides the available dataset into multiple subsets (or folds) and uses different combinations of these subsets for training and testing. This method ensures that the model is evaluated on multiple subsets of the data, providing a more reliable estimate of its performance compared to a single train-test split.

The most common type of cross-validation is k-fold cross-validation, where the data is divided into k equal-sized folds. The model is trained on $k-1$ folds and tested on the remaining fold. This process repeats k times, with each fold serving as the test set once. The overall performance is averaged across all k iterations, reducing the bias associated with a single split.

Cross-validation helps mitigate issues like overfitting or underfitting by providing insights into how the model performs on unseen data. It also allows for better hyperparameter tuning by enabling comparisons of model performance across different configurations. However, cross-validation can be computationally expensive, especially for large datasets or complex models, as the training process is repeated multiple times. For imbalanced datasets, stratified cross-validation is often used to maintain the class distribution across folds. This ensures that each fold represents the overall dataset's characteristics, leading to fairer evaluation metrics, particularly for classification tasks.

Hyperparameter Tuning

Hyperparameter tuning involves optimizing the hyperparameters of a machine learning model to achieve the best possible performance. Hyperparameters are parameters set before the training process begins and cannot be learned from the data, such as the learning rate, regularization strength, number of layers in a neural network, or k in k-nearest neighbors. The simplest method for hyperparameter tuning is grid search, where all possible combinations of hyperparameter values are tested exhaustively. While grid search is thorough, it can be computationally expensive for models with many hyperparameters or a wide range of values. An alternative is random search, which samples hyperparameter combinations randomly and often achieves comparable results with fewer computations.

More advanced techniques, such as Bayesian optimization, use probabilistic models to predict the best hyperparameter values iteratively. This approach focuses on promising areas of the hyperparameter space, making it more efficient for complex models. Similarly, automated machine learning (AutoML) frameworks integrate sophisticated tuning algorithms to streamline the process. Hyperparameter tuning is essential for improving model performance and achieving a good balance between underfitting and overfitting. Poorly chosen hyperparameters can lead to suboptimal results, even with a strong model architecture. Regular monitoring of evaluation metrics, combined with careful selection of tuning methods, ensures the model reaches its full potential.

Overfitting and Underfitting

Overfitting

Overfitting occurs when a machine learning model learns the noise or irrelevant details in the training data instead of the underlying patterns. This results in excellent performance on the training data but poor generalization to unseen or test data. Overfitting typically arises when the model is overly complex relative to the size and quality of the training dataset, such as when using too many features, a deep neural network with excessive layers, or an unpruned decision tree.

Overfitting can be mitigated through various techniques:

- Regularization: Adding constraints to the model, such as L1 (Lasso) or L2 (Ridge) regularization, to penalize overly complex models.
- Dropout: Randomly dropping neurons during training in neural networks to reduce reliance on specific paths.
- Pruning: Reducing the depth or complexity of decision trees to focus on meaningful patterns.
- Data Augmentation: Increasing the diversity of the training data by creating new samples through transformations like rotations, flips, or scaling.

Despite its challenges, overfitting indicates that the model has sufficient capacity to capture patterns, suggesting that careful optimization can lead to better performance.

Underfitting

Underfitting occurs when a model is too simple to capture the underlying structure of the data. It performs poorly on both the training and test datasets because it fails to learn meaningful patterns. Underfitting often happens when the model is too constrained, the training process is insufficient, or the features provided are inadequate to describe the target variable.

To address underfitting:

- Increase Model Complexity: Use a more complex algorithm or increase the number of parameters in the model (e.g., adding layers in a neural network).
- Extend Training Time: Train the model for more epochs or iterations to allow better convergence.
- Improve Feature Selection: Add relevant features or transformations that better represent the relationships in the data.

While underfitting is easier to detect, it indicates that the model needs further refinement to become useful.

Balancing the Two

The challenge in machine learning is to strike a balance between overfitting and underfitting. This is achieved by selecting an appropriate model complexity, ensuring sufficient and diverse training data, and employing techniques like cross-validation to evaluate the model's performance. Regular monitoring of both training and validation errors during training can help identify whether a model is overfitting or underfitting.

Table 6.3: Overfitting vs. Underfitting

Aspect	Overfitting	Underfitting
Definition	Model learns noise and irrelevant details in the training data.	Model is too simple to capture the patterns in the data.
Performance on Training Data	Excellent	Poor
Performance on Test Data	Poor (does not generalize well)	Poor (fails to learn patterns)
Causes	Excessive model complexity, small training dataset, noise in data.	Simple model, insufficient training, poor feature representation.
Solutions	Regularization, pruning, dropout, data augmentation, early stopping.	Increase model complexity, improve features, extend training time.

The above Table 6.3 summarizes the key differences, causes, and solutions for overfitting and underfitting, emphasizing their importance in building well-generalized models.

Conclusion

This chapter highlighted the significance of learning in AI, exploring various types such as supervised, unsupervised, semi-supervised, and reinforcement learning, along with their foundational algorithms. It delved into advanced topics like Markov Decision Processes, Q-learning, and policy gradients while emphasizing the importance of model evaluation and optimization techniques, including cross-validation, hyperparameter tuning, and addressing overfitting and underfitting. Together, these concepts form the foundation for building adaptive, efficient, and robust AI systems.

Exercise

- Explain the concept of learning in AI and discuss why it is important for building intelligent systems.
- Compare supervised, unsupervised, semi-supervised, and reinforcement learning. Provide one real-world example for each type.
- Describe the working principles of Linear Regression and Support Vector Machines (SVM). In what scenarios would you choose one over the other?
- Discuss the differences between K-Means Clustering and Hierarchical Clustering. How would you determine the number of clusters in K-Means?
- Define agents, environments, and rewards in the context of reinforcement learning. Provide an example of how they interact in a self-driving car system.

- Explain the components of an MDP. How does the Markov property simplify the decision-making process?
- Differentiate between Q-learning and policy gradients. What are the advantages of using policy gradients for continuous action spaces?
- What is cross-validation, and why is it important in model evaluation? Compare k-fold cross-validation and stratified cross-validation.
- Describe grid search and random search as methods for hyperparameter tuning. What are the advantages of Bayesian optimization over these methods?

Define overfitting and underfitting. Discuss two techniques for mitigating each issue and their impact on model performance.

Book for Further Reading:

- Artificial Intelligence: A Modern Approach by Stuart Russell and Peter Norvig
- Deep Learning by Ian Goodfellow, Yoshua Bengio, and Aaron Courville
- Machine Learning: A Probabilistic Perspective by Kevin P. Murphy
- Pattern Recognition and Machine Learning" by Christopher M. Bishop
- The Elements of Statistical Learning: Data Mining, Inference, and Prediction by Trevor Hastie, Robert Tibshirani, and Jerome Friedman
- Hands-On Machine Learning with Scikit-Learn, Keras, and TensorFlow by Aurélien Géron
- Artificial Intelligence and Soft Computing: Behavioral and Cognitive Modeling of the Human Brainby Amit Konar
- Reinforcement Learning: An Introduction by Richard S. Sutton and Andrew G. Barto

Bibliography

- Anwar, K., Siddiqui, J., & Saquib Sohail, S. (2019). Machine Learning Techniques for Book Recommendation: An Overview. *SSRN Electronic Journal*. https://doi.org/10.2139/ssrn.3356349
- Anwar, K., Siddiqui, J., & Sohail, S. S. (2020). Machine learning-based book recommender system: A survey and new perspectives. In *International Journal of Intelligent Information and Database Systems*. https://doi.org/10.1504/IJIIDS.2020.109457
- BOZKURT, O. (2023). Inhuman Power: Artificial Intelligence and the Future of Capitalism. *Lectio Socialis*. https://doi.org/10.47478/lectio.1162633
- Burkov, A. (2019). The Hundred-Page Machine Learning Book-Andriy Burkov. In *Expert Systems*.
- Feldman, A. (2006). Computational Linguistics: Models, Resources, Applications. *Computational Linguistics*. https://doi.org/10.1162/coli.2006.32.3.443
- Girasa, R. (2020a). Artificial intelligence as a disruptive technology: Economic transformation and government regulation. In *Artificial Intelligence as a Disruptive Technology: Economic Transformation and Government Regulation*. https://doi.org/10.1007/978-3-030-35975-1
- Girasa, R. (2020b). Artificial Intelligence as a Disruptive Technology. In *Artificial Intelligence as a Disruptive Technology*. https://doi.org/10.1007/978-3-030-35975-1
- Goodfellow, I., Bengio, Y., & Courville, A. (2016). Deep Learning - whole book. *Nature*.
- Goodfellow, Y. B. A. C. I. (2015). Deep Learning Book. In *Deep Learning*.
- Groote, J. F., & Tveretina, O. (2003). Binary decision diagrams for first-order predicate logic. *Journal of Logic and Algebraic Programming*. https://doi.org/10.1016/S1567-8326(03)00039-0
- Hastie, T., Tibshirani, R., & Friedman, J. (2009). machine learning book. *Elements*.

- Hemphill, T. A. (2019). Book review: Prediction Machines: The Simple Economics of Artificial Intelligence. *Journal of General Management.* https://doi.org/10.1177/0306307019854812
- Jebari, K., & Lundborg, J. (2019). The intelligence explosion revisited. *Foresight.* https://doi.org/10.1108/FS-04-2018-0042
- Kaperonis, S. (2023). How Artificial Intelligence (AI) is transforming the user experience in digital marketing. In *The Use of Artificial Intelligence in Digital Marketing: Competitive Strategies and Tactics.* https://doi.org/10.4018/978-1-6684-9324-3.ch005
- Kedia, A., & Rasu, M. (2020). Hands-On - Python Natural Language Processing. In *Packt Publishing.*
- Kim, K. G. (2019). Deep learning book review. *Nature.*
- Koprowski, R., & Foster, K. R. (2018). Machine learning and medicine: book review and commentary. *Biomedical Engineering Online.* https://doi.org/10.1186/s12938-018-0449-9
- Kucirkova, N., & Mackey, M. (2020). Digital literacies and children's personalized books: Locating the 'self.' *London Review of Education.* https://doi.org/10.14324/LRE.18.2.01
- Lana, M. (2022). Artificial Intelligence Systems and problems of the concept of author. Reflections on a recent book. *JLIS.It.* https://doi.org/10.36253/jlis.it-468
- Lidströmer, N., & Ashrafian, H. (2022). Artificial Intelligence in Medicine. In *Artificial Intelligence in Medicine.* https://doi.org/10.1007/978-3-030-64573-1
- Lu, J., Ou, C., Liao, C., Zhang, Z., Chen, K., & Liao, X. (2021). Formal modelling of a sheet metal smart manufacturing system by using Petri nets and first-order predicate logic. *Journal of Intelligent Manufacturing.* https://doi.org/10.1007/s10845-020-01602-0
- MEHAN, J. E. (2022). Artificial intelligence – Ethical, social, and security impacts for the present and the future. In *IT Governance Publishing.*
- Mosco, V. (2019). The Laboring of Artificial Intelligence [Book Review]. *IEEE Technology and Society Magazine.* https://doi.org/10.1109/mts.2019.2948417
- Neapolitan, R. E., & Jiang, X. (2018). Neural Networks and Deep Learning. In *Artificial Intelligence.* https://doi.org/10.1201/b22400-15
- Popenici, S., Rudolph, J., Tan, S., & Tan, S. (2023). A critical perspective on generative AI and learning futures. An interview with Stefan Popenici. *Journal of Applied Learning and Teaching.* https://doi.org/10.37074/jalt.2023.6.2.5

- Salukhe, A. (2023). Elements of the Theory of Computation. *International Journal for Research in Applied Science and Engineering Technology*. https://doi.org/10.22214/ijraset.2023.53969
- Sethy, A., Rout, A. K., Uriti, A., & Yalla, S. P. (2023). A comprehensive machine learning framework for automated book genre classifier. *Revue d'Intelligence Artificielle*. https://doi.org/10.18280/ria.370323
- Shaalan, K. (2011). Book Reviews Introduction to Arabic Natural Language Processing. *Acm Transactions On Asian Language Information Processing*.
- Sirignano, J. A. (2019). Deep learning for limit order books. *Quantitative Finance*. https://doi.org/10.1080/14697688.2018.1546053
- Smith, S. J. J. (2005). Empirical methods for artificial intelligence [Book Review]. *IEEE Expert*. https://doi.org/10.1109/mex.1996.546589
- Tegetmeier, C., Johannssen, A., & Chukhrova, N. (2023). Artificial Intelligence Algorithms for Collaborative Book Recommender Systems. *Annals of Data Science*. https://doi.org/10.1007/s40745-023-00474-4
- The international dictionary of artificial intelligence. (2000). *Choice Reviews Online*. https://doi.org/10.5860/choice.38-0036
- Wang, D., Tan, B., Wei, M., Cui, X., & Huang, X. (2023). Using natural language processing and machine learning algorithm for book categorization. *Applied and Computational Engineering*. https://doi.org/10.54254/2755-2721/2/20220551
- Wang, H., Czerminski, R., & Jamieson, A. C. (2021). Neural Networks and Deep Learning. In *The Machine Age of Customer Insight*. https://doi.org/10.1108/978-1-83909-694-520211010
- Wang, Z., Du, P., & Yu, Y. (2009). An intelligent modeling and analysis method of manufacturing process using the first-order predicate logic. *Computers and Industrial Engineering*. https://doi.org/10.1016/j.cie.2008.10.003
- Wen, W. (2022). Research on Modern Book Packaging Design Based on Aesthetic Evaluation Based on a Deep Learning Model. *Scientific Programming*. https://doi.org/10.1155/2022/8329745